MW00452022

Money from Mobiles

D. Rod Lloyd

Copyright 2019

About the Author

 My name is Rod Lloyd. I was born in Southport England in 1954 which makes me 62 years old as I write this book. This book is written as a hands-on landlord. I am not an English major or represent to be a literary specialist, just an average Joe that owns rental property.

My grandfather [on my mother's side] was a gentleman farmer and a shrewd business man. He died age 92 when I was aged 7. He had purchased about a handful of modest single-family rental houses over his years. My working-class family lived in one and paid my grandfather rent. My dad was a shipping clerk in Liverpool. My mother was a homemaker and I had two older sisters.

After my grandfather died, my mother and her sister inherited the rentals and his home. Our house and my grandfather's house were sold and we bought a larger home for our growing family. That left about 5 rentals to be managed. These were kept and managed by my mother, mainly because her sister lived out of town. So

I grew up with the landlord in my blood and property management in my face.

In England in those days, kids could leave school at 15 years old. When I turned 15, I was offered an apprenticeship by a family friend who was a self-employed Carpenter and Joiner. A Carpenter does rough framing woodwork while a Joiner does finish woodwork and cabinet making. In those days, power tools were rare. My boss had NO power tools. Wood was cut with various hand saws, holes drilled by a brace and bit, wood was smoothed and profiled by all manner of planes and chisels.

The apprenticeship was a day-release program where I worked 4 days a week on the job and attended the local trade school one day and evening per week.

This was really a 3-year trade school program to attain the City and Guild qualification, but no one ever told me that. At the end of each year I signed up for the next until after 10 years, I sat and passed the Higher National Diploma in Building, which was administered by the Royal Institute of British Architecture in London.

After completing my 5-year apprenticeship, I continued on as a journeyman Carpenter and Joiner but my feet were itchy with all that education. I landed a job as assistant Building Inspector in Liverpool, about 20 miles away. I was making good money and was getting ambitious. I asked my mother if I could buy one of her rentals. We worked out a deal with my mother and her sister and I became a landlord. I sold it a few years later for a tidy profit.

I moved to the USA in 1981 at the age of 27. I had put an ad in the LA times, looking for a place to stay in exchange for work around the house. Merry answered my ad and I moved to the US into Merry's spare bedroom. I remodeled her kitchen with ease and she was impressed with my skills.

I quickly got a job as a carpenter for a property company. One man owned 462 rental units in LA in 13 buildings all within a few blocks of each other in the Wilshire district. I was the only carpenter on a team with 4 painters, 1 plumber/electrician, and one handyman. Take note of the staff ratio and I will discuss this later on. I soon became familiar with US rental property and their maintenance.

I had moved on from Merry's spare bedroom into my own apartment but Merry kept in touch with me. She offered to a partnership with me on a house flip. Her father put up the money and we purchased an odd looking home in the fancy Studio City area and turned it into the best on the block. When sold, there was enough profit to make a down payment on a home. Oh by the way, by then Merry and I were married. I guess I did not read the fine print in our partnership agreement.

I moved on from my Carpenter position to start a Home Inspection service. In those days, Home Inspections were a new industry in the US in the 80's but I was familiar with the concept from England and I had a lot of inspection experience. I got in on the ground floor.

The realtor that handled the house flip found a duplex foreclosure. The bank wanted 10% down and provided the financing and a 20-day escrow. We bought it, I got it into shape and we rented it out for a nice little cash flow. That was followed by a tri-plex foreclosure. We scraped the money together for the down payment. I got it into shape and rented them out.

We were next offered a fourplex foreclosure. We went to look at it and it was a super deal, but Merry pointed out a small detail, **we had no more money** for the down payment.

Merry called a friend who was impressed with what we had been doing. The bottom line is they became 50-50 partners. They borrowed the money for the down payment and fix up cost. A couple of years later we sold the property. Our friends had enough to put a down payment on a condo and we had enough to put a down payment on 11 crappy units.

From there we decided LA was not the place to raise my young family and we decided to liquidate and move to Kelseyville on the banks of Clear Lake in Northern California.

We bought 24 apartment units and ran them for a while then liquidated and bought a 24 space mobile home park with 545 ft. of lakefront property. We lived on that glorious property as the kids grew up. When our 3 kids turned 18, there was no sign of them moving out, so **we moved out**. We moved again north to Rainier Oregon and eventually liquidated the mobile home park.

I now am buying rental property nearby. I manage the property and do all the maintenance.

Money from Mobiles

Introduction

This is a nuts and bolts description of how to make money from mobile homes. I have no intention of talking you into this plan by giving brainwashing example after example of the deals. I am also not going to gloss over the pitfalls and problems of the system either. It is not a get rich quick scheme and there is some risk involved. It takes some cash to run the system and I do not recommend doing on a shoestring. It takes some time but can be a lot of fun.

However, it is possible to make a very good return on your investment. Today interest rates have almost shriveled up and died. Those who have saved all their lives to have a secure retirement have a wakeup call from failed speculative investments or almost zero interest rates for the safe investments.

This is a no fluff description of how it works. You will need to make adjustment to the numbers to fit where you live and the changing economy. The main thing is to understand the method in a concise and straightforward way.

The Basic Concept

With mobile homes, it is a fact that most buyers have little or no money. That is the nature of mobile home owners. They are content living in mobiles because it is the cheapest form of housing but gives a modest amount of dignity and independence in owning your own home.

When a mobile homeowner wants to sell however, they also ways want cash to get on with the next part of their life. This leaves a gap in the market. Sellers want cash, but the buyers do not have cash and the banks will not lend on older mobiles.

This is where you come in. You have some capital and you want to make a fair return on your investment. You will be excited to make 10% interest on your money and the mobile homeowners will be happy to pay it. So, by playing bank, you can easily make money lending to mobile home buyers with the mobile home as collateral.

There is more room to make profit if you want to purchase the mobile with the power cash gives you and resell to the new owners with the benefit of easy qualify financing.

I want to say right up front that I do not recommend renting out a mobile home. They are constructed differently than stick built apartments and houses, and they do not stand up to the rough treatment of many renters. When you sell a mobile, the owners have a pride of ownership missing from renters. They will take better care of the unit and they will hold their value better.

When you agree to purchase a mobile, make the deal contingent on being approved by the park, and have the seller state in writing that everything is working and there are no roof leaks.

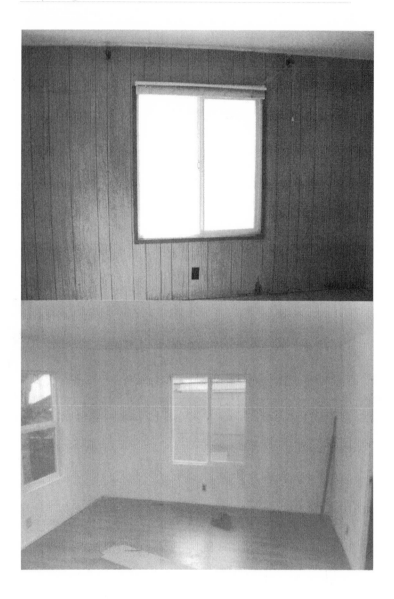

Let's look at a Typical Deal

1970 one bedroom mobile 12 by 40 advertised for $5,000. That is a very typical asking price for an older unity that size. The power of cash allows you to make a fair offer of $4,000 knowing you do not have to buy but they do have to sell to someone. Do not gouge your seller but hold out for a fair discount. Make sure you get clear title before completing the deal.

Once you are the owner, step back and look to see what a potential buyer will see. Make sure it looks clean and tidy from the front. Do some painting if necessary and add a few flowers. Tidy up the skirting. Paint the front door a strong contrasting color.

Make sure the interior is tidy - no trash, blinds open and tidy. Walls: clean, paint if necessary. The carpet has been cleaned or replace with laminate flooring. The kitchen must look tidy. Paint the cabinets if necessary or even upgrade the doors, hardware and faucet.

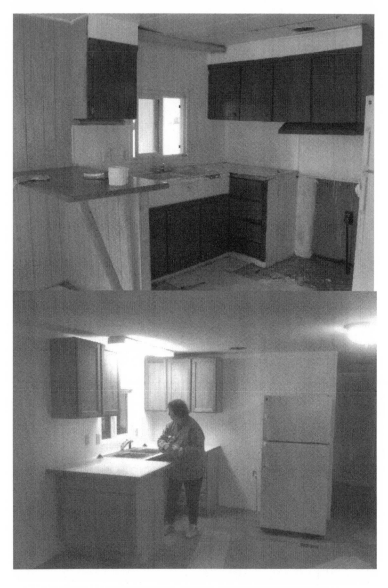

The bathroom must look clean. Add caulking or
replace the tub surround if necessary. If you can do

the work yourself, plan on spending $500 on materials. If you need to pay a handyman, plan on $1,000.

So, we now have $5,000 into the unit. It will likely sell for $8,000 to $10,000 sold with easy financing. So how much do we make?

The monthly payments will be $290.40 for a three-year loan at 10% interest with $1,000 down. The profit is:

$290.40 per month
36 payments
$10,454 total from payments
$1,000 down payment
$11,454 total income [loan and down payment]
Your investment is:
$4,000
$1,000 fix up
$1,000 less deposit
$4,000 total
Your return is 2.8 times your investment in three years or 95% per year.
The system is as simple as that, but you do need to know the downside.

As soon as you become the owner of the unit you are obligated to pay the site rent and you must be approved by the park to keep your mobile home in the park, so before you commit to buy, you must talk to the park manager about this.

It is perfectly possible you will be able to sell the unit within 30 days but if it takes three months, you might well be out another $1,000 in space rent. The deal will still make a good profit, but you must understand this.

In my example above, I use the deposit amount of $1,000. Most buyers will have a hard time with this but if you take less, say $500, there is a very real chance that sooner or later you will never see another penny and you will need to evict them. Eviction takes time and you will lose money if this happens. Once the eviction is complete, you can resell it and chances are you will still come out ahead, but you will be soured by the deal. The point being, you need $1,000 down unless you extremely comfortable with your new buyer.

Let me make it clear, once you sell a unit, the new owners must maintain the unit and pay the space rent, so you have nothing to do but collect money.

You will need to keep good bookkeeping, calculate the remaining balance and issue the 1098 to the buyer for the interest paid during the year.

In order to protect your investment, you will need to make a condition of purchase that insurance be kept on the unit. This is not very expensive, and I prefer to buy the insurance and add it to the loan, than rely on them to buy it and keep it up. Put all this in your purchase contract together with a due-on-sale clause. Add the cost of the insurance to the loan payment.

Negotiating a Sale

There are several elements to a sale.
Price
Monthly payment
Interest rate
Length of loan
Down payment
No two potential buyers are the same. Some will get hung up and the interest rate, others on the sale price. The point being, find out how much they can afford each month and structure a deal around that. A smaller payment would mean a longer term. Lower sales price could increase the interest rate.

If the potential buyers like the unit but are unhappy with the carpet or some other feature, work with them to buy that item and add the cost to the loan.

Make sure your contract to sell indicates it is an **AS-IS** sale.

Own the Park

The very best way to work this system is to own the mobile home park. Find a park that has a lot of vacant sites. That park is likely to accept a low purchase price. Then hunt down good deals and have the units moved to your park. If the park has over-nighters or short-term rentals, convert it to full-time units. Short term rentals make more per night but when you take into consideration the time the sites are vacant and the extra work in checking and out the overnighters, it usually works out better to have full-timers.

When the park is full of permanent units, the rent is just about guaranteed. If someone wants to move, they must sell the unit and pay the site rent and any loan, until an approved new owner is found, or you can buy the unit back for cash at a discount and resell at a full price with easy financing. Unlike owning apartments, there is no maintenance calls. Each tenant maintains their own unit. All the benefits of rental real estate, without the headaches.

You might find the park owns some of the units and rents them out. This is great, offer to sell the units to the tenants, for the same price as renting. No more repairs and when they want to move, they must sell and find someone new with no interruption of site rent. Of course, you can provide the financing if needed.

Licensing and Permits

Unlike stick-built housing, mobile homes are regulated by HCD. Housing and Community Development. You need to become familiar with their licensing and permit requirements. If your work with them they can be easy to get on with. If you do not work with them, they can become a nightmare. Visit the web page for the HCD in your state.

In some states, mobiles are registered by DMV as personal property, but in other states they are registered by HCD. You need to research how mobiles are registered in your state and what the process and fees are.

Repairs

My favorite repair to a mobile is to rip up the old smelly carpets and put down the inexpensive laminate flooring. If you plan on replacing the carpet, you will need to pay a carpet installer to install it correctly, which can cost more than the cost of carpet, but you can install laminate flooring yourself and save a bundle. The unit looks great when it is done, and it can reinforce any soft areas in the floor. You need to know, when the buyers move in with their furniture, not much of the floor will show, but when it is empty, the floor is the biggest visible item. Laminate flooring is easy to install, it just clicks together and makes the unit pop.

If the carpet is good but the particle board floor below has become wet, it will need to be patch repaired. Peel the caret back. Cut a piece of 3/4" plywood just a bit bigger than the wet area, then place the plywood down over the area and draw a line around the plywood. Cut out along the line and break out the old flooring. Add 2x4 supports underneath if necessary and screw down the plywood and put the carpet back.

If the roof leaks, you can spread a product called "snow roof" over the leaking area. Be sure you put extra around the flashings. It is best to use a roof primer first.

If the ceiling has stains, be sure you paint it before you put the new floor down. Use a good primer on any stains so they do not bleed through. If the wall panels are good, just give it a good cleaning and remove any nails. If it is bad, paint the paneling again before you put down the flooring. Be sure you paint the closets also.

I have plenty of time on my hands and I like to take off the paneling and install drywall and texture. It is not necessary, but I get a much higher resale price and drywall is cheap.

The kitchen and bathroom must look smart. This is a make or break item in a sale. It is very easy to remove old cabinet and replace with stock units from the big box store for a few hundred dollars. Take out the old cabinets, fix the ceiling and walls and paint, put in the laminate flooring then the kitchen cabinets, and it will look sharp.

If something is needed, and I have what is needed in my house, I will often use mine in the mobile and buy a new better item for my home (mirror, light fixture, rug, stove, fridge etc).

An alternative is to offer to sell As-Is and buy the fix-up materials and add the cost to the loan - less work and more interest.

Marketing

The first thing to do is put a sign in the front window. Also put an advert in the throwaway neighborhood newspaper. These ads are cheap, and this is where your customers look first. Put an ad in Craigslist. This is free. Make sure you mention at the top, **Seller Financing**.

Create a web page if you can and put the address on all marketing. Then put all the information and lots of photos on the web page. Play with the verbiage. They are mostly interested in how much down and how much a month. You will be surprised how few people will negotiate the price or terms. Get an application and small deposit from those interested and run a credit app on them.

When not to buy

Do not buy a mobile:
That must be moved (unless you want to place it somewhere else)
That has roof leaks

That has electrical problems
That does not have a title or clear title
That has a tenant in it
That is overpriced. You must have room to make a
profit.
That has an illegal addition.

If They want to Sell

Many times, they will want to sell before the loan is paid off. Make sure you have a due on sale clause in the purchase contract. You have choices if they do.

One: you can buy back for the outstanding balance of the loan. This means you get to keep the deposit and any principal they have paid.

Two: you can let the new buyer assume the loan with new down payment.

Three: you can negotiate a new loan with the new buyer.

Four: you can do nothing and maybe you will end up getting the unit back when they walk.
In any case, you come out a winner.

Research

It is very important to research mobile prices in your area. Search out every park and every mobile for sale in your area. Look inside every mobile for sale and keep track of prices. Use this information to determine the fair market value of mobiles so you will know a good deal from a porker.

The Big Fear

A lot of people considering this plan are afraid the owner will move out or stops paying. When you transfer the title, you will make sure you are listed as lien holder. That way you can take the mobile back if necessary and sell it to someone else for even more profit.

If you are not sure, go find a mobile but do not buy, take an advertisement out in the paper with you increased price indicating seller financing and see how the phone rings. Then go make your deal and then show to your leads. All you have to lose is the cost of a small ad and you have so much to gain.

So...... What are you waiting for!

History

Mobile homes or static caravans (also informally called "caravans" or "trailers") are prefabricated homes built in factories, rather than on site, and then taken to the place where they will be occupied. They are usually transported by tractor-trailers over public roads to sites which are often in rural areas or high-density developments. In some countries, they are used for temporary accommodation on campsites.

While these homes are usually placed in one location and left there permanently, they do retain the ability to be moved, as required in many areas. Behind the cosmetic work fitted at installation to hide the base, there are strong trailer frames, axles, wheels, and tow-hitches.

In the United States, this form of housing goes back to the early years of cars and motorized highway travel. It was derived from the travel trailer, a small unit with wheels attached permanently, often used for camping. Larger units intended to be used as dwellings for several months or more in one location came to be known as home trailers. The first trailer home originated from England where they are called "caravans".

The original rationale for this type of housing was its mobility. Units were initially marketed primarily to people whose lifestyle required mobility. However, beginning in the 1950s, the homes began to be marketed primarily as an inexpensive form of housing designed to be set up and left in a location for long periods of time, or even permanently installed with a masonry foundation. Previously, units had been eight feet or less in width, but in 1956, the 10-foot wide home ("ten-wide") was introduced, along with the new term "mobile home".

The homes were given a rectangular shape, made from pre-painted aluminum panels, rather than the streamlined shape of travel trailers, which were usually painted after assembly. All of this helped increase the difference between these homes and home/travel trailers. The smaller, "eight-wide" units could be moved simply with a car, but the larger, wider units ("ten-wide", and, later, twelve-wide") usually required the services of a professional trucking company, and, often, a special moving permit from a state highway department.

During the 1960s and '70s, the homes were made even longer and wider, making the mobility of the units more difficult. Nowadays, when a factory-built home is moved to a location, it is usually kept there permanently, and the mobility of the units has considerably decreased. In some states, mobile homes have been taxed as personal property if the wheels remain attached, but as real estate if the wheels are removed.

Many people who could not afford a traditional site-built home or did not desire to commit to spending a large sum of money on housing began to see factory-built homes as a viable alternative for long-term housing needs. The units were often marketed as an alternative to apartment rental. However, the tendency of the units of this era to depreciate rapidly in resale value made using them as collateral for loans much riskier than traditional home loans. Terms were usually limited to less than the thirty-year term typical of the general home-loan market, and interest rates were considerably higher. In other words, mobile home loans resembled motor vehicle loans more than traditional home mortgage loans.

Sizes

Mobile homes come in two major sizes, single-wides and double-wides. Single-wides are 18 feet (5.5 m) or less in width and 90 feet (27 m) or less in length and can be towed to their site as a single unit. Double-wides are twenty feet or more wide and are 90 feet (27 m) in length or less and are towed to their site in two separate units, which are then joined together. Triple-wides and even homes with four, five, or more units are also built, although not as commonly. They also differ from site-built homes in that it is not uncommon for owners of single-wides to "trade up", as one might with a car.

While site-built homes are rarely moved, single-wide owners often "trade" or sell their home to a dealer in the form of the reduction of the purchase of a new home. These "used" homes are either re-sold to new owners or to park owners who use them as inexpensive rental units. Single-wides are more likely to be traded than double-wides because removing them from the site is easier. In fact, only about 5% of all double-wides will ever be moved.

Regulation

In the United States, these homes are regulated by the U.S. Department of Housing and Urban Development (HUD), via the Federal National Mfd. Housing Construction and Safety Standards Act of 1974. This national regulation has allowed many manufacturers to distribute nationwide because they are immune to the jurisdiction of local building authorities. By contrast, producers of modular homes must abide by state and local building codes.

There are, however, wind zones adopted by HUD that home builders must follow. For example, state-wide, Florida is at least wind zone 2. South Florida is wind zone 3, the strongest wind zone. After Hurricane Andrew in 1992, new standards were adopted for home construction. The codes for building within these wind zones were significantly amended, which has greatly increased their durability. During the 2004 hurricanes in Florida, these standards were put to the test, with great success. Yet, older models continue to face the exposure risk to high winds because of the attachments applied such as carports, porch and screen room additions. These areas are exposed to "wind capture" which apply extreme force to the underside of the integrated roof panel systems, ripping the fasteners through the roof pan causing a series of events which destroys the main roof system and the home.

Legal complications

The popularity of the factory-built homes caused complications the legal system was not prepared to handle. Originally, factory-built homes tended to be taxed as vehicles rather than real estate, which resulted in very low property tax rates for their inhabitants. This caused local governments to reclassify them for taxation purposes.

However, even with this change, rapid depreciation often resulted in the home occupants paying far less in property taxes than had been anticipated and budgeted. The ability to move many factory-built homes rapidly into a relatively small area resulted in strains to the infrastructure and governmental services of the affected areas, such as inadequate water pressure and sewage disposal, and highway congestion. This led jurisdictions to begin placing limitations on the size and density of developments.

As noted above, early homes, even those that were well-maintained, tended to depreciate in value over time, much like motor vehicles, rather than appreciate in value, as with site-built homes. The arrival of these homes in an area tended to be regarded with alarm, in part because of devaluation of the housing potentially spreading to preexisting structures.

This combination of factors has caused most jurisdictions to place zoning regulations on the areas in which factory-built homes are placed, and limitations on the number and density of homes permitted on any given site. Other restrictions, such as minimum size requirements, limitations on exterior colors and finishes, and foundation mandates have also been enacted. There are many jurisdictions that will not allow the placement of any additional factory-built homes. Others have strongly limited or forbidden all single-wide models, which tend to depreciate in value more rapidly than modern double-wide models.

Apart from all the practical issues described above, there is also the constant discussion about legal fixture and chattels - meaning that the legal status of a trailer is, or could be, affected by its incorporation to the land or not. This sometimes involves such factors as whether the wheels have been removed.

◊ Mobile homes are often sited in land lease communities known as trailer parks. Also referred to as trailer courts, mobile home parks, mobile home communities, manufactured home communities, and factory-built home communities, these communities allow homeowners to rent space on which to place a home. In addition to providing space, the community can provide basic utilities such as water, sewer, electricity, or natural gas and other amenities such as community rooms, pools, and playgrounds.

There are over 35,000 trailer parks in the United States ranging in size from 5 to over 1,000 home sites. Although most parks appeal to meeting basic housing needs, some communities specialize towards certain segments of the market. One subset of mobile home parks, retirement communities, restrict residents to those age 55 and older. Another subset of mobile home parks, seasonal communities, are located in popular vacation destinations or are used as a location for summer homes.

Newer homes, particularly double-wides, tend to be built to much higher standards than their predecessors and meet the building codes applicable to most areas. This has led to a reduction in the rate of value depreciation of most used units.

Additionally, modern homes tend to be built from materials similar to those used in site-built homes rather than inferior, lighter-weight materials. They are also more likely to physically resemble site-built homes. Often, the primary differentiation in appearance is that factory-built homes tend to have less of a roof slope so that they can be readily transported underneath bridges and overpasses.

Modular built homes are transported on flatbed trucks rather than being towed, and lack axles and an automotive-type frame. However, some of these homes are towed behind a semi-truck or on a frame similar to that of a trailer. The home is usually in two pieces and is hauled by two separate trucks. Each frame has five or more axles, depending on the size of the home. Once the home has reached its location, the axles and the tongue of the frame are then removed, and the home is set on a concrete foundation by a large crane.

Both styles are commonly referred to as factory-built housing, although its technical use is restricted to a class of homes regulated by the Federal National Mfd. Housing Construction and Safety Standards Act of 1974.

Bill of Sale
And Promissory Note

I _____ do hereby
purchase a Mobile Home _____; located
_____
_____ for the purchase price
of $_____ date _____.

Buyer has had a full opportunity to inspect the mobile home and is purchasing it in AS-IS condition.

The purchase price [$_____] is to be paid in monthly installments. not less than $_____ due and payable on the first of each month until paid in full. Interest shall be added at the rate of _____% until paid in full. A $25.00 late charge will be added to any payment received after the 1st of the month.

The buyer is responsible for all transfer and registration fees. Fire insurance must be obtained and kept in force for the term of this loan for at least the amount of the loan with _____ named as additional insured.

Failure to provide proof of insurance, the seller may obtain insurance at buyer's expense and add it to the loan amount. The loan shall be paid in full if the mobile is sold or moved from the park.

Buyer   **Date**   **Date**

Seller   **Date**   **Date**

Buying and Running a Profitable Mobile Home Park

You have probably been driving by Mobile Home Parks for years and not giving them a second thought, let along thinking of buying a park but I am going to give you skinny all about owning a Mobile Home Park, the good, the bad and the ugly.

The general impression people have about mobile home parks is they are cheap, nasty untidy housing units with low income, low educated tenants. I am sure you feel you have nothing in common with mobile homes or their tenants.

I have to admit, I have a strong prejudice .... For green money

What is a Mobile Home Park?

If you have heard the term **Cash Cow**, that's about the best description I can give most Mobile Home Parks, with the right management.

Mobile Home Parks function just like a city subdivision, but a privately-owned subdivision. In many respects, the owner of the park makes the laws. They decide who lives there, how much the space rent is, when quiet hours are, if it is senior only or open to families, parking, laundry etc etc.

Just to clarify what is a mobile home park. It can be called a trailer park, mobile village, trailer court, RV park and several other names. They all mean the same thing.

They are not regulated by the city or county however, they are regulated by the owner and overseen by the state (Housing and Community Development). In some states, DMV handle the title of ownership and other states it is controlled by HCD.

There are a few cities that have been given the power to oversee the regulation of Parks, but these are rare and it makes little difference to the park owner.

There are rules for the size of the roads, lighting, sewer, water and electric. There are rules about the sites and how the mobile home is sited on the lot, and parking etc etc.

Park owners operate by the issuance of a permit to operate issued by the state, and it specifically indicates how many sites you are licensed for.

Once the park has a current permit to operate, you can install mobile homes. Homes under a certain size do not need to have a permit to install. They can be built up to 400 square feet. Dimensions are usually 12' x 30' (not including porches). Over that size, they do need a permit to make sure the setbacks are correct and the stairs to enter the home are safe.

Once a unit is set and approved by the state, the unit can be sold and occupied. The occupants can either buy the unit and pay space rent to the park owner, or rent the unit and pay rent to the unit owner. The unit owner would pay space rent to the park owner if the unit is not owners by the park.

Some park space rent includes some or all the utilities, but most do not, and the tenant needs to have the electric / gas / water meter service put in their name. This system is best for the park owner, but it also keeps the space rent lower and the tenant has control of the utility charge.

New Parks

In order to create a new park, first the city or county planning must approve a planning application. This will depend on the zoning and you should talk to the planning department directly first.

Once approved by the planning, it needs to be approved by the state HCD and you should talk to the state early on in your design stage. Plans will be needed to show the park layout conforms to the state regulations. This is like creating a subdivision and it is not for the faint of heart.

Existing Parks

If you are considering purchasing an existing park, this will be much easier than creating a new park. The transaction is similar to purchasing any other piece of real estate.

Before you commit to a purchase, check with HCD to ensure it has a current permit to operate and there are no outstanding violations against the park. Also check the number of actual sites does not exceed the approved number of sites.

Next get a list of the site rents and determine how many sites are occupied and determine the actual income and potential income if the park is not fully occupied.

Next get a list of the expenses which will include:

Property tax (this might change when you purchase)
Insurance
Electric
Water
Trash
Gas
Manager
Maintenance
Office expenses

Make sure the numbers given to you seem reasonable and verify them where possible.

Now you can subtract the expenses from the income to determine the net profit (before and loans)

From this you can determine if it is a good investment to purchase.

Space Rents

It might be the space rents are low and you might be able to increase the income. At this point you need to do research with all the other parks nearby to see how full they are and what the typical rents are.

If indeed you are lower than the competitors, you might have a good opportunity to increase the space rent and increase profits. Watch out though, if the other parks have higher rents but are not full, that might happen to you and you might end up losing tenants and losing more money. This is called power and consequences.

I have always found it best to be a little under the going rate, have a full park with happy tenants is much better than the aggravation of trying to maximize profits and having a lot of headaches in the process.

Advantage of a Mobile Home Park

The biggest advantage a mobile home park has over an apartment building or houses with tenants is the maintenance, or lack of it. Basically, all you are renting is the dirt, or the ground the mobiles sit on. The ground does not need much if any maintenance. You will be responsible to maintain the sewers, water pipes, any gas lines etc. You will be amazed how the tenants can screw up a sewer. However, it is relatively easy to have sewers rooted and often you can charge the tenant the cost.

Watch out for a park that has septic tanks however. They can be a nightmare. Also 50-year-old parks will have 50-year-old water pipes which can be a problem. Take all this into consideration when you consider purchasing a park.

On-Site Manager

The larger parks will need to have an onsite manager. It might only be a discount in rent to have someone on site to handle problems, but the very large parks will need a full-time manager with an office.

Never under any circumstances get into the situation where tenants pay a manager cash.

In fact, it is best in all cases to have an all check policy with no exceptions. Tenants without a bank account can use money orders. Tenants that give bad check must use money orders also.

The manager can show vacant sites and units to potential tenants. They can keep the park tidy and do basic maintenance to the common areas. Accept rent checks etc etc. They basically take the weight of park ownership off the park owner.

Vacant Sites

When I bought my first park, it was 25 spaces and half of the spaces were empty. That is why I got a good deal on the park, but it was not a positive cash flow at half full. So, I did a lot of advertising and within a year I was down to one vacant site. The problem was, all the new tenants had RV's (recreational vehicles) mobiles that were too mobile, ie travel trailers and motorhomes etc. So every time I rented the last space, another would become vacant again, and I was losing potential rent.

Finally, I decided to buy a used double wide to fill the last space. I made a good deal with the mobile home mover to buy the unit and have it installed. Once it was ready and signed off by the inspector, I advertised it with easy financing.

It was sold very quickly, so I did the same thing every time a space came available. Soon, the tenants in the old single wides wanted to trade up to the nicer double wides. We hauled away the old single wides and installed the nice used double wides, with higher space rents and 10% interest over 7 years. The tenants were so happy to get more space for their growing families, they hugged me, and I am so not a hugger, but it felt good that they liked the deal so much. It was the old win-win.

Within a couple of years, my park was full, looked great, the tenants were very happy, and I was making a nice profit.

Things to Know if you are Creating Loans

It is very important you make it a condition the tenant get insurance, enough to cover the loan and to haul away the unit if it burns out.

The contract must include a due on sale clause, in case the owners want to sell the unit to someone else. You may well agree to allow the new owners to continue the loan with a new down payment, but you must have the right to approve the new owners first.

Make a condition that the loan becomes due on move if the mobile moves out of the park, becomes delinquent with the space rent or they violate the park rules.
Sell As-IS

The Down Side to Owning

The nature of a mobile home park is tenants living very close to each other. Human nature dictates there will be friction. Playing music too loud, dogs barking, parking in the wrong space, a lot of visitors, garbage not put out, trash in the front yard, leaving clothes in the laundry washer, painting the outside of their mobile a gaudy color, not keeping their lot tidy, grass cut, kids playing in the street, you name it, it will happen.

The owner becomes the mayor of the community and gets to try and resolve these disputes and keep order. You need to be a firm diplomat. You need a lot at patience and self-control. You need a good set of park rules and enforce them.

Collecting the Rent

It is harder to evict tenants in a mobile home park, and for good reason. It is not as easy for tenants to pick up and move as it is with an apartment. If you evict a tenant, they will have to pay $2,000 to $3,000 to move their unit, and much more if they have carport, shed, deck, double-wide addition etc. Rent collection for a mobile home park needs a new landlord mentality.

Fact is, you have a captive audience. The best of intentioned by the tenants will fall astray from time to time. Be sure you have a strong late penalty clause in your contract and enforce it. Surprisingly, they will pay the extra charge and it works out to be well worth your extra work. I will take late charges all day long.

I do let the tenants know that payment history is considered at the end of the year when I am deciding on space rent increases. The best payers get little or no increase. The habitual late layers get the biggest increase. They usually move on soon enough.

In ten years, I have only had to do one eviction, two eighteen-year-olds. I should have known better when I agreed to rent to them. That was my stupid money and I quickly got over it. When I owned apartments, I was in court every other month with one eviction or another.

Be fair with the tenants. Be consistent. Bend a little when needed. Have a big summer picnic. Become their friend, not their enemy. Know their names and kids. Look out for the older folks. Keep the common areas neat and tidy.

RV Sites

Some parks are licensed for overnight RV spaces. The rules are a little different for these including needed public bathrooms and showers, etc. Overnight spaces generate much more income per night, but they require much more supervision and staffing, and the times when the spaces are vacant can quickly make it more trouble than they are worth. My recommendation is to stick with full-timers.

Water Meters

Most parks were set up with just one master water meter for the whole park. This is license for abuse and lack of maintenance. It is very easy to screw off the faucet, add a meter and put the faucet back on. Meters cost about $35 and will pay for themselves the first month or so. I read the meters every other month and add the cost to the rent. The average water bill is $40 to $60 per site and you will soon see how the main water usage will go down.

Repairs

Most parks have a handyman. By that I mean a tenant who is able to do small jobs and repairs, in exchange for a little income. Find out who is the handyman in your park and set them up mowing the grass, blowing the leaves, changing light bulbs, trimming branches etc etc. This is win-win.

Following are sample :

Move-In Procedure
Park Rules and
Rental Agreement
Adjust them to suit your park

Move-in Procedure

This guide is made out to help your move go easier.
This page is not park rules.
Make contact with the following, as you require.
Give them as much notice as possible so the service
will be on when you move in.

1 Contact Power Company to have the electric
turned on 1 800 _____.

2 Contact Cable TV if you require Cable - 1 800
_____.

3 Broadband internet is also available from
_____.

4 Contact your Satellite TV service. You will need
management permission for location of any new
dish. Dish Network or Direct TV are good.

5 Contact the phone company for telephone service.
1 800 _____. You may need to install a post for
them. [Cell phone reception is good in the park.]

6 If there is a gas tank for your space, contact the
company that owns the tank and arrange to take
over the service. If there is no tank, you will need to
make your own arrangements for gas service if
required. You will need management permission for
the tank location. All gas installations MUST be
safe upon connection.

7 Mail is delivered to a "gang" box at the street in front of the property. You need to go to the thee Post office to set up your mailbox. You may need to show your rent receipt to prove you are moving in.

____Mobile Home Park - Rules & Regulations
The Management of the _____ has
established the following Rules and Regulations,
which apply to all residents and guests for the
benefit of all tenants. These rules ~~may me~~ *may be*
modified by the Park Owner without notice.

A. MOBILE HOME

1 Storage of any items underneath any mobile home is prohibited.

2 Storage of items behind or around your site shall be kept to a minimum and subject to the consent of the management.

3 No appliances, or furniture not intended for outside use may be placed outside.

4 Utility, sewer cleanouts and water meter/shutoffs must be kept readily accessible at all times.

5 Guests and visitors are the responsibility of the tenant with whom they are visiting whether by invitation or not.

B. CONDUCT

1 Actions by any person of any nature, which may be dangerous or create a health and or safety problem or disturb others, are not permitted. This includes but is not limited to: any unusual, disturbing or aggressive noise, intoxication, quarreling, threatening, fighting, immoral or illegal conduct, profanity, or rude boisterous, objectionable or abusive language or conduct.

2 No open containers of alcohol are permitted within the Mobile Home Park except within a mobile home space.

3 Radios, television, stereos, musical instruments and other devices must be used as to not disturb others.

4 Quiet hours are to be observed from 10:00 pm to 8:00 am. Noise must be kept to within your own rental space within these hours.

5 Children must be quiet and orderly and not be allowed to play in the street unsupervised, other resident's property without them being present and consenting, or do anything, which might disturb the quiet enjoyment of other residents. Tenants shall be solely responsible for their children and guest children.

C. MOBILE HOME MAINTENANCE AND REPAIR

1 Residents shall maintain their mobile home and all structures, trees, improvements and their things attached to or placed thereon in good condition and repair, in a neat, clean and well-kept manor.

2 Mobile homes must be kept weather tight at all times. Tarps placed over roofs must be limited to 21 days and roof repairs be made as soon as possible.

3 Tenant is responsible for all water piping on you site after the meter.

4 Tenant is responsible for all sewer pipes from the ground connection.

5 Tenant is responsible for all electrical connections and fittings past the site outlet.

6 When resident is away, it is residents responsibility to have someone maintain their mobile home and lot. If the absence is over 2 weeks, management should be notified.

7 If any portion of the mobile home or its accessory structures or equipment is damaged, the repairs must be completed within two [2] weeks. This includes but is not limited to: damage to the siding, awnings and supports, downspouts, stairs, decks, skirting, porches, windows or storage sheds.

8 Management must approve in writing prior to starting any work including but not limited to: additions, fences, decks, sheds, carports, porches, patio's, additions, exterior wiring or lights, exterior painting, tree cutting or pruning, propane tank, fuel oil tank, stairs, docks, pilings etc,

9 Tenants parking cars and mobile homes under or near trees assume all risk of falling leaves, branches etc.

10 Fences will not be approved having a height more than 36" in the front half [nearest the road] of the lot and 60" in the rear half of the lot without Park approval.

11 Anything, which creates a hazard to health and safety, shall not be permitted. No flammable, combustible or explosive fluid or material, chemical, or substance except ones customarily used for normal household purposes may be stored in the space and then only in suitable marked containers in quantities necessary for normal household purposes.

12 Existing shrubs or trees may not be removed from the premises.

13 Residents shall bear the cost of repairs to any utilities or Park property damaged by the resident. To avoid damage to underground facilities, residents must have Management permission prior to digging or driving rods or stakes into the ground.

14 The Park is served by septic tank draining. Because of this there are certain precautions necessary as follows: Only biodegradable toilet paper may be used; Only normal human waste and water may access the drainage system; No sanitary napkins may be placed down the toilet. Abuse to the draining system will render the Resident liable for the cost of rooting and pumping of the drains and septic tank.

D. DOCKS AND SHORELINE

1 There are no lifeguards on duty. Use facilities at your own risk. An adult registered tenant must accompany all guests and young children.

2 Management has the right to refuse use or close areas to anyone at any time.

3 Pick up all trash and debris. Keep area's clean during and after your use.

4 Use of the launch ramp is limited to tenants and tenant's guests while tenant is present. Tenant's guest must have prior permission from management. Use by non-residents is prohibited. Use of the ramp is at your own risk. The ramp is subject to closure at management's discretion.

5 Parking of boat trailers must have management prior written approval. Additional fees may apply.

6 Resident understands that the Mobile Home Park fronts Clear Lake, which is likely to flood into the property from time to time rendering some spaces inaccessible during times of flooding. Resident understands that the Park accepts no responsibility for damage to the Residents mobile home or personal property in the event of flooding. During flooding, it

may be necessary for Management to close portions of the Park. In such case, space rent will still be payable without discount. Residents are urged to obtain insurance to include flooding.

E. PETS

1 Special written permission to keep house pets in the park must be obtained from the management prior to obtaining the pet. A house pet is defined as a pet that spends its primary existence within the mobile home. The management reserves the right to deny a resident a pet if there are an excessive number of pets in the park. The management's decision in this matter is final.

2 Small dogs may be considered. All dogs must be licensed and have rabies shots. Tenant must show proof on request. Pit Bulls or similar are not permitted.

3 All cats must be spayed / neutered and wear a collar ID. Tenant must show proof on request.

4 Dogs must be on a leash and the leash held by its owner at all times outside the mobile space. Any pet running loose in the park may be impounded at the owners expense and the resident tenancy may be terminated.

5 All pet excrement left by the pet must be picked up immediately and properly disposed of.

6 If a pet causes disturbance, annoyance or harm, such as barking, growling, biting or any other unusual noise or damage, permission to keep the dog will be revoked.

7 Guest's will not be allowed to bring their pets into the park.

8 No exterior pet housing is permitted in the park.

9 Tying pet outside the mobile home and leaving unattended is prohibited.

F. AUTO AND PARKING

1 STATE LAW PROHIBITS ON-STREET PARKING. Park only on your own space. Residents are NOT permitted to park in the guest parking areas, in vacant spaces, on other mobile home spaces or other common land. Vehicles violating these policies will be towed at owners expense CVC22658.

2 Vehicles are not allowed into the park if they are not in normal, safe, operating condition or not currently DMV registered.

3 Repairing of vehicles in the park is not permitted.

4 You must park on your own site. **Tenants must not park in Guest Parking**. There is a $5.00 charge per day/night or part of a day/night for violations.

5 Management reserves the right to limit guest parking to prevent overcrowding.

6 Speed limit in the park is 5 MPH. All vehicles must stay on the paved roadway and not go around the speed bumps.

G. GARBAGE

1 Tenants must store all trash in approved trash containers and be emptied weekly. Tenants must not accumulate any trash. The management shall have sole discretion in determining this. Trash cans may not be taken to the parking lot until after 9pm Sunday and must be removed before 5 pm Monday.

H. GENERAL

1 These rules and regulations become part of the rental agreement along with the California Civil Provisions Mobile home Residency Law, which is revised every year. They are legally binding documents that govern the conduct and agreement between mobile home landlord and tenant.

2 The Park is private property and under state law, it is the responsibility of the owner of private property to enforce State Law.

3 Violation of State Law, County Codes, or Park Rules and Regulations may result in termination of tenancy.

4 The park management shall be the sole judge of whether a park rule has been violated and what action if any should be taken.

5 Using the excuse that others break the same or similar rules will not be an excuse for any tenant to also break the rules.

6 The park, management and tenants should all be on the lookout for each other's property. However, the park in no way offers any formal or informal security for your mobile home or possessions. Each tenant is urged to take out insurance and install security lighting.

7 Guest may not stay more than 7 consecutive nights or a total of 21 nights per year without Park Owner written permission.

8 Rent is due on the first and late after the first. Rent paid after the first shall be subject to a $25.00 late charge. If the first is a weekend or public holiday, rent may be paid on the first business day after the first without a late charge. Three-day notices may be

issued when the rent is not paid by the 10th. **You may request an emergency short delay is paying rent but this will only be approved if you have a previously timely payment history**. Past late payment history shall not establish an approved history and a change in the payment date.

Standard Mobile Home Space
Rental Agreement

Park   Name: _____ **,**

_____

Effective Date _____ **,**
Space Number: _____ **;**

Responsible Tenants Name _____ **;**
Beginning Rent $ _____

The following persons listed below are approved and authorized to reside in the designated space, agree to be bound by and subject to all the terms of this agreement and are referred to in the balance of this document as "Resident". The Lakewood Park Resort will be referred to in the balance of this document as "Park".
A [Adult]; P [Pet]; C [Child] - enter age if under 18

[ ] _____
[ ] _____
[ ] _____
[ ] _____
[ ] _____
[ ] _____

UTILITIES & SERVICES: Utilities & Services to be **provided** by the Park for Residents during the term of this agreement. Water and sewer is billed separately by the park which may be increased based on actual cost. In the event the cost of such services increase, the resident agrees to pay such increase as soon as it occurs. Utilities & Services **NOT provided** by the Park include but is not limited to Electric; Gas; Propane; Phone; Cable, Trash, internet. Tenant must contract with Timberline Disposal for trash pickup within 2 weeks of move-in. The park will bill you additionally for your water/sewer usage every two months.

TERM: The term of this agreement shall be Month-to-Month, beginning on the date specified above and continued **until terminated in writing by either party having given not less than 60 days written notice**, in accordance with the provisions of the Mobile home Residency Law and any other applicable law. Resident understands that they have the option to have a fixed term lease instead of a Month-to-Month tenancy.

RENT AND OTHER CHARGES: Residents shall pay rent specified above or as amended, per month on or before the 1st day of each month, commencing at the start of the term of this Rental Agreement. In addition, Residents shall pay the utilities and other charges billed by the Park to the Resident on or before the 1st day of each month. Payment for either rent or other charges must be paid without deduction or offset whatsoever. The late charge shall be $25. Payment will be made to the on-site manager or given/mailed directly to the owner.

ADMINISTRATIVE CHARGE: A charge may be assessed by the Park in the amount of $25.00

whenever rent and other charges are paid after the due date. This charge will also apply whenever a check for rent or any other charges is returned unpaid from a bank or other financial institution [each time]. When payment is made no matter how specified, it will first be credited towards any outstanding deposit, then any late rent or charges and finally to current rent.

INSTALLATION AND REMOVAL The tenant shall be responsible for all installation, moving, and leveling, re-leveling, installation permit and removing for mobile homes. Foundations and supports should be adequate to support the mobile home. Any re-leveling after flooding is also the responsibility of the tenant. Tenants assume all risk of falling trees, leaves, branches etc. including any damage to parked cars and mobile homes under or near trees

PARK RULES: The current Park Rules are a part of this Rental Agreement and are incorporated herein by reference as though fully set forth at this point. Resident agrees to comply with all the Park Rules that now exist and such additional Rules as may be promulgated by the Park from time to time in accordance with the in Accordance with the provisions of the Mobile home Residency Law and any other applicable law. I have received the Park Rules.

MOBILEHOME RESIDENCY LAW: Resident hereby acknowledges receipt of the Mobile home Residency Law, a part of the Civil Code of the State of _____, a copy of which is attached hereto. Terms and provisions of the Mobile home Residency Law are specifically made a part of this Rental Agreement, and are incorporated herein by reference as though fully set forth at this point. The tenant is responsible for any violations for their own site and uncorrected violations will be grounds for termination of the tenancy.

COMMON FACILITIES: It is the responsibility of the Park to provide and maintain the physical improvements in the common facilities of the Park in good working order and condition. With respect to a sudden or unforeseeable breakdown or deterioration of the physical improvements in the common facilities, management shall have a reasonable period of time to repair the sudden or unforeseeable breakdown or deterioration and bring the improvements into good working order and condition after management knows or should have known of the breakdown or deterioration.

SITE MAINTENANCE: The Park may charge a reasonable fee for services relating to the maintenance of the land and premises upon which the Mobile home is situated in the event the Resident fails to maintain such land or premises in accordance with the Rules and Regulations of the Park after written notification to the Resident and the failure of the Resident to comply within fourteen [14] days. The written notice shall state the specific condition to be corrected and an estimate of the charges to be imposed by the Park if the Park or its agent performs the services.

ANIMALS: No animals shall be brought onto the Park without prior written approval from the Park. In the event one or more dogs are approved, they must be kept inside the mobile home and not fenced or chained outside. Under no circumstances may any dog be allowed to roam free within the park.

Excessive barking as determined by the Park is prohibited and grounds for prohibiting any dog on your premises. Dogs taken for walks must be restrained on a leash of reasonable length and kept under control. No more than two cats may be owned by any Resident [per site].

DRAINS: Resident understands the Park is served by septic tank draining. Because of this there are certain precautions necessary as follows: Only biodegradable toilet paper may be used; Only normal human waste and water may access the drainage system; No sanitary napkins may be placed down the toilet. Abuse to the draining system will render the Resident liable for the cost of rooting and pumping of the drains and septic tank.

CHANGES IN RULES, STANDARDS OF MAINTENANCE, SERVICES, EQUIPMENT, OR PHYSICAL IMPROVEMENTS: The Park's Rules & Regulations, standards of maintenance of physical improvements in the Park, together with services [including utilities], equipment and physical improvements within the Park may be changed from time to time as provided by the Park, the Mobile home Residency Law and any other law then in effect.

ENTRY UPON RESIDENT'S SPACE: The Park shall have a right of entry upon the land on which a mobile home is situated for maintenance of utilities, maintenance of premises if the occupant fails to do so, and the protection of the Mobile home Park at any reasonable time. However, such entry shall not be in a manner or at a time, which would interfere with the occupant's quiet enjoyment. The Park may enter a mobile home without prior written consent of the occupant in the case of an emergency or when or when the occupant has abandoned the mobile home.

TERMINATION OF RENTAL AGREEMENT BY RESIDENT: The Resident having given **60 days written notice may terminate this Rental Agreement.** Resident understands that this Rental Agreement will remain in effect and Resident will be liable to pay rent as set forth in this Agreement whether or not Resident occupies the home site/space. This Rental Agreement will remain in effect for the 60-day period of notice and until the mobile home and all personal items/trash are removed, or upon approval, occupancy and payment in full of rent and deposit of new Resident in the event the Mobile home is sold onsite.

TERMINATION OF RENTAL AGREEMENT BY PARK: This Rental Agreement at the option of the Park may be declared forfeited and/or the tenancy may be terminated and/or Residents right to possession terminated in accordance with the Mobile home Residency Law and any other applicable law. Any such rights granted the Park due to any amendments, deletions, or modifications of the Mobile home Residency Law and the Park may enforce other applicable laws.

REMOVAL ON SALE: The Park may, at its option, in order to upgrade the quality of the Park, require the removal of the mobile home from the Park upon its sale to a third party, in accordance with the provisions of the Mobile home Residency Law and any other applicable law. Any rights granted the Park due to amendments, deletions or modification of the Mobile home Residency Law and any other applicable law may be enforced by the Park.

APPROVAL OF PURCHASER AND SUBSEQUENT RESIDENTS: Resident may sell his or her mobile home at any time pursuant to the rights and obligations of the Resident and Park under the Mobile home Residency Law and any other applicable law. Resident must however, immediately notify the Park in writing of Resident's intent to sell his or her mobile home if the prospective purchaser intends for the mobile home to remain in the Park.

If the Park does not exercise its rights pursuant to the Mobile home Residency Law to require the removal of the mobile home from the Park, and in order for the prospective purchaser to reside in the Park, he and/or she must [1] complete an application for tenancy; [2] be accepted by the Park; [3] execute a new Rental Agreement; [4] sign and deliver to the Park a copy of the Park's then effective Rules and Regulations.

RENTING OR SUBLETTING: Resident shall not sublease or otherwise rent all or any portion of Resident's mobile home or the premises. Resident shall not assign or encumber his or her interest in this Rental Agreement or the premises. No consent to any assignment, encumbrance, sublease or other renting shall constitute a further waiver of the provisions of this paragraph.

If Resident consists of more than one person, a purported assignment, voluntary, or by operation of law, from one person to the other shall be deemed an assignment within the meaning of this paragraph. In the event the mobile home is not the Resident's primary residence, members of their family may occupy the mobile home for short periods after giving written notice to the Park indicating the names and dates involved.

USE PROHIBITED: The mobile home and premises shall be used only for private residential purposes and no business or commercial activity of any nature shall be conducted thereon without prior written approval from the Park.

IMPROVEMENTS: All improvements must be submitted in writing to the Park and no work may start before this work is approved by the Park. All plants, shrubs, and trees planted on the premises as well as all structures, including fences, decks, landscaping, pilings embedded in the ground, if allowed in the Park or lake adjacent to the Park, pursuant to the Rules and Regulations, blacktop, concrete or any structures permanently attached to the ground, shall become the property of the Park as soon as they are installed and may not be removed by the Resident without the prior written consent of the Park. Resident shall maintain all of the above at Resident's sole expense and responsibility and shall be completely responsible for each of them although they are the property of the Park. The Park may remove them at its option.

FLOODING: Resident understands that the Mobile home Park fronts Clear Lake, which is likely to flood into the property from time to time rendering some spaces inaccessible during times of flooding. Resident understands that the Park accepts no responsibility for damage to the Residents mobile home or personal property in the event of flooding. During flooding, it may be necessary for the Management to close portions of the Park. In such case, space rent will still be payable without discount. Residents are urged to obtain insurance to cover flooding.

WAIVER: The waiver by the Park of, or the failure of the Park to take action in any respect because of any breach of a term, covenant or condition contained herein or the violation of a Park Rule or Regulation shall not be a waiver of that term or rule. The subsequent acceptance of rent or other charges by the Park shall not be a waiver of any preceding breach of this Rental Agreement by the Resident or any violation of Park Rules or failure of Resident to pay a particular rent, regardless of the Park's knowledge of the preceding breach or violation of Park Rules or Regulations or failure to pay rent.

ATTORNEY'S FEES AND COSTS: In any action arising out of Resident's tenancy, this Agreement, or the provisions of the Mobile home Residency Law, the prevailing party shall be entitled to reasonable attorney's fees and costs. A party shall be deemed a prevailing party if the judgment is rendered in his or her favor or where the litigation is dismissed in his or her own favor prior to or during the trial, unless the parties otherwise agree in the settlement or compromise.

TIME OF THE ESSENCE: Time is of the essence of this agreement.

INTERPRETATION: Each provision of this Rental Agreement is separate, distinct and individually enforceable. In the event any provision is declared to be unlawful or unenforceable, the validity of all other provisions shall not be affected.

INSPECTION OF PREMISES: By signing this Rental Agreement, Resident acknowledges that

Resident has carefully inspected the space to be rented and all the Parks facilities and has found them to be in every respect as represented by Park to the Resident either orally or in writing, and to the extent that they are not exactly as represented, either orally or in writing, accepts them as they are.

EFFECT OF THIS AGREEMENT: Resident agrees that this Rental Agreement contains the entire Agreement between the parties regarding the rental of the home site/space within the Park.

ALTERATION OF THIS AGREEMENT: This Agreement may be altered only by written Agreement by both of the parties, by operator of law, or in any manner provided for by the Mobile home Residency Law and any other applicable law. The Park may modify the Park Rules at any time without notice.

ACKNOWLEDGMENT: Resident acknowledges that he and / or she has received a copy of this Rental Agreement, together with a copy of the Park Rules and Regulations and a copy of the Mobile home Residency Law and further, that he and/or she has read and understood each of these documents. Resident understands that by signing this Rental Agreement, he and/or she will be bound by its terms and conditions thereof.

_____   _____

Signed Tenant date   signed park date

PARK * ACCOUNT SUMMARY

Originated:				Original Amount:		5,000.00
Borrower:				Interest Rate:		10%
Address:						
Property:	Mobile Home					

HISTORY OF ACCOUNT BALANCE

Due Date	Late Charge	Interest	Principal	Pre-Paid Amount	Total Payment	Remaining Balance	Comments
3/1/2011	-	33.33	260.18	-	293.51	4,739.82	
4/1/2011	-	31.60	261.91	-	293.51	4,477.91	
5/1/2011	-	29.85	263.66	-	293.51	4,214.25	
6/1/2011	-	28.10	265.41	-	293.51	3,948.84	

SECTION III

Profitable Rental Property Investing

Introduction

In this section, I will focus on buying real estate for a rental investment with that mindset - "Buy and Hold". It is likely the property will sell for a nice profit sooner or later but we will focus on the rental market and its present return. For this reason, the property selection will be different from the house flipping section of this book and the fix-up process will be different.

I have combined this with the house flipping because the two subjects have a lot in common, and many times a project that starts out as one turns into the other. There will be some repetition from the first section for those who only want to do one or the other.

The similarities include the property selection process, preparation, and upgrades ready for the new tenants, with some obvious or not so obvious modifications.

The process must be conducted as a business, in a very professional manner. The more preparation you do, the more work you will save and the more money you will make.

I will present you some concepts that are controversial and collide with conventional wisdom. I do this on purpose. Those who follow

the crowd, do so at their own peril. I ask that
you keep an open mind.

Why Economy Rental Property

There have been more fortunes made from real estate than any other form of investment, and you don't need a degree in business or finance to jump on this bandwagon.

There are very few safe investments, and until the Housing Market Crash of 2007, real estate was a slam dunk to increase over time. After the real estate crash, we were given a wake-up call. Those who were heavily leveraged [financed] found themselves underwater, meaning they owed more on the loan than the property was CURRENTLY worth.

For the seasoned investors, this did not hurt us. As long as one did not have to sell during the real estate depression, there was no loss, after all, rents and expenses stayed the same, in fact, as homeowners were foreclosed upon, they needed a place to rent, the foreclosure inventory went up and the purchase prices went down. To the rental investor, this is good news, an investors bubble.

Some Property Examples

I am going to take some real property listed for sale in my town at the time of writing [2014]. You will find the numbers surprisingly low compared to maybe your area. All the concepts scale up, or you could look a little further afield to find deals like mine.

1st Deal [low end]

164 18th Ave, 2 beds, 1 bath, 938 sq. ft. listed for sale at $39,900. I would offer $30,000 on this home and not pay a penny more than $35,000. We will use the number $35,000. It is currently rented for $475 and the tenant wants to stay. It should rent for at least $100 more but I would leave the tenant in place and defer the inevitable vacancy and fix up cost. The tenant pays all utilities so I would only need to pay property tax [$621/12] =$51.75 plus insurance [$500/12] =41.66. This leaves a positive cash flow of $381.59 [475-51.75-41.66]. Paying all cash gives me an annual return of $4,579.08 or 13.08%.

2nd deal [mid range]

506 16th Ave, 3 beds, 1 bath, 1,014 sq. ft. listed for sale at $105,000. I would not pay any more than $95,000. This is a few blocks up the street but in a much better part of the town and is bigger. It is likely to rent for $875. The tenant pays all utilities so I would only need to pay property tax [$1,219/12] =$101.58 plus insurance [$800/12]=66.66. This leaves a positive cash flow of $706.76 [875-101.58-

66.66]. Paying all cash gives me an annual return of $8,481.12 or 8.92%. Compared to #1 above at 13.08%, the second deal is not as good value.

3rd deal [high range]

2220 Cascade Way, 3 beds, 2 baths, 2,120 sq. ft. listed for sale at $249,900. I would not pay any more than $200,000. This is in the best part of town in a very desirable neighborhood.   It is likely to rent for $1,675. The tenant pays all utilities so I would only need to pay property tax [$3,177/12]   =$264.75   plus   insurance [$1,600/12] =133.33.   This leaves a positive cash flow of $1,276.92 [1,675-264.75-133.33]. Paying all cash gives me an annual return of $16,523.04 or 7.66%. Compared to #1 above at 13.08%, and #2 at 8.92 the third deal is not as good value.

Time and time again, the cheapest homes in town make the most money, plus you can buy much more for your money, diversifying your risk. If you own one large rental and it becomes vacant, you lose all your rental income. If you have 5 smaller rentals, you make more, even if one is vacant.

If you finance the transaction with say 20% or 25% down, the numbers are still comparable.

Do that calculation for yourself. That is why I recommend economy rental property.

The Math – How you make a Profit

It might seem obvious that the profit comes from the rent you collect, and that is true, but it is not the whole story by any stretch of the imagination.

We will start by identifying the two methods of purchase.

- o All Cash
- o Financing

By paying all cash, most of the rent you collect will be profit – after property taxes, insurance, utilities, repairs etc. The problem with all cash is it takes a lot of it. By taking out a loan [mortgage] with say 20% down, you can buy 5 times more property using OPM [Other People's Money]. We will see some financial comparisons between the two later on.

There are also two types of rental property:

- o Single-Family Dwelling [house]
- o Multi-Family dwelling [apartments]

We will focus for now on the single-family dwelling.

We said earlier that we make money from the rent. Actually, we make money from what is left over from the rent after paying the bills, but there is more money to be made than that. There are actually four [or more] ways to make money.

1. **Cash Flow.** This is as stated above, what is left from the income after paying the bills.

2. **Capital Appreciation.** This means that if the property goes up in value over time, it eventually will be a source of income when you sell – Capital Gain.

3. **Principal Reduction.** Assuming you have a loan which is covered [paid] by the income, the tenants are actually paying for most of the building. As you pay principal and interest, the loan balance goes down over time. When you come to sell, this principal reduction will also make you money.

4. **Tax Benefits.** There are many tax benefits from owning a business and especially rental property. Talk to your accountant about these benefits.

All that is a mouthful but when you think about it, it is a win, win, win, win.

1. Cash Flow

Deal with Financing		
Address	344 21st Ave, Longview	
Asking Price	54,900	
Estimated Sales Price	40,000	
Initial Fixup	2,000	
Down payment + Fix-up	25%	12,000
Loan Amount		10,000
Interest Rate/2nd 5 yr	3.50%	264.00
Closing Cost/Total Cash	3,122	**15,122**
Mortgage Payment		135.00
Property Taxes	384	32.00
Insurance	600	50.00
Maintenance [estimated]	19	19.00
Utilities	0	0.00
Total Expenses		**500.00**
Estimated Rent Income	700	700.00
Net Cash Flow		**200.00**
Return on Investment		15.87%

In this example, you will see that the Asking price was $54,900 but the seller [the bank as a foreclosure] took the offer of $40,000. The rent is $700 and the expenses add up to $500 leaving a cash flow of $200 which relates to a 15.87 return on investment. Each year you can raise the rent. Watch what your nearby rents are charging and make an annual adjustment [up] to increase your cash flow.

2.   **Capital Appreciation.**

In the above example, if the property is purchased for $40,000 and eventually it is sold in say 5 years for $80,000 in a stronger market which is a 200% gain or 40% per year.

3. Principal Reduction.
Using the above 5 years example, assuming a 15-year loan, after 5 years the loan balance will be $21,688 meaning a net profit of $8,312. This represents 18% of the original investment per year. The longer you own it, the faster the principal goes down.

3.   Tax Benefits
There some strange tax benefits to rental property investment established by the IRS, and it is possible to save 10% on your existing tax liability.

If you add all these benefits together, you get a whopping return on your investment. Even if you make little or no cash flow the first year, you are still generating equity which is the current value of the investment minus the current loan balance.

Passive vs Active Management

Passive real estate investing is where you buy a rental property and have a professional property management company manage it. You are 'hands off'. They find the tenants to move in, they do the paperwork, they supervise the maintenance of the property, they evict the deadbeats and they send you a check for the profit [hopefully] at the end of each month.

Active real estate investing is where YOU manage the property, you are 'hands on'. You find the tenants to move in, you do the paperwork, you do or supervise the maintenance of the property, you do or supervise evicting the deadbeats.

There is a stigma about being a landlord, having to clean other people's mess, repairing their damage, begging for the rent, taking legal action when they do not behave. That is why real estate investment makes such good money. We deserve it.

So, if a professional property management company will do all the work for us, why would we want to volunteer to do the nasty work ourselves?

Property management companies do a great and professional job of running a rental property. They are licensed real estate agents and of course, they charge for their service. This is money out of your pocket.

They are obligated to maintain the property to a high and professional standard, to protect themselves [from lawsuits] and maintain your investment. They usually have a few maintenance workers on staff and they charge for everything. The tendency is for them to spend most if not all your profit. No one looks after your money like you do.

If you are a doctor or lawyer or other high paid professional and want a hands-off investment, this can work very well. For the rest of us, I strongly recommend doing the management yourself.

From an income tax point of view, active management has more tax benefits than passive management, but you need to explore that with your accountant.

The Skills You Need

If you hired a plumber to install a water heater, you would expect that plumber to be skilled in plumbing and you would expect he had installed many water heaters before and own all the tools and know what parts to bring.

If you went for a job interview for an accountant, the employer would expect you to have college training in accountancy and understand the skills of bookkeeping and general accounting.

If you want to become a landlord, you need to understand buildings and building maintenance or the repair costs will eat you alive.

Consider being a landlord a 'Mom and Pop' business. It is a 'hands-on' job. Paying professionals to do all the repairs and hiring contractors to remodel a unit between tenants will cost you ALL your profit.

You might think it is easy for me to preach doing all your own maintenance when I am a builder. The fact is, 90% of the work needs very little skill and is easy to learn. Most people can haul trash to the dump, clean and paint. Most people can learn how to repair a running toilet, replace a faucet, change locks, upgrade light fixtures, and repair holes in walls. If you read my chapter "About the Author" you will know I am a trained carpenter [only 5% of the work is carpentry], the rest I am self-taught. I figured out what I needed to know, as and when I needed it. Read on and I will guide you to learn what you need to know.

I will allow you to have ONE fear trade. One item you just won't go there. It might be plumbing, maybe electrical. You must do everything else but that. I will not accept a long list of I can't do this and I won't do that. If that is your deal, find another business.

Your best friend is YouTube. You can lean most anything by watching YouTube videos. When I was learning my other trades, I did not have the benefit of YouTube.

Sidebar

Recently I had a bedroom window that would not stay open and the new tenant was moving in the next day. It had been upgraded to a modern vinyl window before I purchased the property but this vertical slider would not stay open. I looked hard at the window. I know how to fix the weights on wood windows but had no clue with the new vinyl windows. I knew there was a spring somewhere that must be broken but could not see where it was or how to repair it. I called my local glass/window company and asked how much they would charge to fix my problem. They told me it would be $80 labor *plus parts and they could not come out until next week.*

I went on YouTube and found a demonstration of removing the same kind of sash [sliding part of the window] exposing the spring, and how to replace it.

I then followed the instructions, took the old spring to my local glass company. I bought a new pair of replacement springs for $18 and had it back installed all within an hour. I saved $80 or put it another way, I earned $80 for one hours work and now I know how to make this repair in the future.

I try to do all my own repairs and upgrades, but carpet is not a job I ever mastered. It is not hard to get down and cut to size, but the stretching, joining and making it look good always eluded me. Besides, carpets and tenants do not seem to be compatible.

I can have a new carpet in my home and it looks fine for decades with proper care and cleaning. Many tenants, however, do not respect carpet. Chances are a new carpet when a tenant moves in, will need replacing when they move out, even after two years.

This was the case with a three bedroom apartment that I had just evicted the tenant. I inherited the unit carpeted but it was toast when the tenant moved out. Home Depot had a whole house installation special for $35 plus the cost of the carpet. This seems like a great deal but when I did the math, it was going to cost over $600 to carpet the three bedrooms using inexpensive carpet.

My preference is to install laminate flooring. Home Depot has an inexpensive line for 69 cents a sq. ft. I bought 280 sq. ft. of this flooring for under $200. It took 16 hours for me to install. I saved over $400 or earned $25 per hour. I also know the laminate floor will likely survive 10 to 20 years even with tenants and I think it looks nicer. It won't need shampooing when they move out, just a light mopping and it looks like new.

The bottom line is I want you to have the attitude that owning a rental property needs 'hands-on' effort to be profitable. If this is your income or part of your income, treat it like a business. You need to take the time to learn these skills. You need to do **everything**. Read on, I will teach you all the basics.

Later on, I will likely contradict myself on this subject. Let's call them exceptions to the rule, and I will explain why when I get to them. This will give me time to think of why they are exceptions.

Merry has a cousin who is her best friend. She lives across the country and they have long phone conversations. She is a brilliant math wizard and when I first met her, she taught college-level math.

I told her about real estate and she was intrigued. Next thing I know, she bought 16 units nearby and she was off and running. She used her math skills to analyze the market and cash return. She is quite wealthy but a bit of a tightwad [I mean this in the kindest way in case she reads this book]. She does all her own maintenance and upgrades. Painting, plumbing, kitchen upgrades. She does everything except electrical. That is her one Opt Out, which is fine.

When her son was going off the college [MIT] I suggested she buy a small apartment building for him to live in and manage for four years. She liked the idea and bought a fourplex. Even with him taking one of the units, it made a small profit, enough to pay for his books. When he graduated, they sold the property and netted $100,000 [split 50-50] and his lodging was free.

Tenants respect a hands-on owner

I met a mobile home park owner. She said he hated every one of her tenants, and they hated her. I decided she was in the wrong business. It did make me think, though.

Later that day, as I walked around my own mobile home park, many of my tenants made warm comments to me, and I realized that most if not all my tenants liked me, and I liked them also. So what was the difference?

I pondered that and decided it was two factors:

1. I did my own maintenance. They saw me out there fixing this and that, hauling away trash in my truck, being involved with the tenants.
2. I was firm but fair with everyone. The park rules were clear and I enforced them equally to each tenant. I was polite to everyone but did not allow anyone to take advantage of me.

On the other hand, a landlord that drives up in a fancy car, demands rent and leaves without putting anything back into the property is disliked.

Time is money

I hear landlords all the time saying

"Time is Money"

"I don't have time to spend in trivial painting…I can pay someone to do that."

The fact is, every penny you spend on labor is money out of your pocket. I recommend you make your mind up you will be the labor [husband and wife/family]. The fact is if you set up your rental property correctly and it becomes your income, that is what you are getting paid to do. No one will take care of your property like YOU.

Maximizing Profits

For the sake of this discussion, I am going to assume you are purchasing a single Family Dwelling, which your research tells you it will rent for $1,000 per month. You got a great price because it needs some work and escrow will be closing soon.

Its earnings potential is $1,000 per month or $12,000 per year gross [before expenses]. That is $33.33 per day. But you have to do some remodeling before it can be rented. Every day you spend remodeling the property, you are losing $33.33, [$1,000 divided by 30] so you need to get the remodeling done as quick as possible.

The remodeling will take labor and materials. If you plan on doing the work yourself, let's assume you think it will take no more than one month. That means you are losing $1,000 gross income during the fix-up. Let's say the materials will cost an additional $500. By the time it is ready to rent, you have a loss of $1,500, not to mention the tax, insurance, and utilities.

If you hire a contractor who can bring in a crew and knock off the work in one week instead of your month, and the contractor charges you $3,000 labor and $900 materials [contractors always seem to mark up the materials], your loss would be $3,900 plus the week of lost rent, $33.33 x 7 =$233.31 totaling $4,133.31. In this scenario, you are much better off doing the work yourself even though it will take longer.

This is just an example of course. Every time you think about hiring someone to do work on your rental, go through the numbers. In almost all cases, you are better off doing the work yourself. Every dollar you spend on labor is a dollar out of your profit.

An added bonus of doing the work yourself is you can advertise the unit for rent and be on site to show it to potential renters. Chances are you will have a renter all ready to move in the day you finish work.

Now, this brings up a common objection. For some reason I do not comprehend, many landlords refuse to advertise and show the unit until all the work is complete. Nine times out of ten, I am able to rent the unit while still being fixed up. Why lose that marketing time. The fact is once I have a renter, I hustle to get it finished. If I do not get a renter early on, I spend a little more time making improvements until it does rent.

Sweat Equity

When you buy a property, you pay for the purchase and you no longer have your money, but you have equity in the building, meaning it has value other than liquid money. You could sell it or trade it or use it to make money as in rent it for a profit.

If you pay all cash to buy your building, you have 100% equity [in simple terms]. If you put 25% down and take a mortgage for 75%, you have 25% equity in the building. As you pay down the mortgage, your equity goes up in direct proportion to the principal you pay off.

You can gain equity in more ways than simply paying for the building in cash or paying down the mortgage. If you study the market in your area and are able to move fast with a cash offer, you can "buy low". By solving one person's problems, a quick sale with no contingencies, you can buy property for less than it is worth. Being in a position of correcting negative property features that make a property not qualify for a mortgage, then correcting the problems, you make the property more desirable and you immediately create 'sweat equity'.

By correcting objectionable features like a dated kitchen or bathroom or irradiating a mold problem, or a trashed property with graffiti, holes in walls, you create 'sweat equity'.

By taking a property that is the worst on the block and turning it into the best on the block, giving it curb appeal, you create 'sweat equity'.

By taking on a partner that pays for the property while you fix up and manage it, you create 'sweat equity'. Your labor is transformed into equity by increasing the value of the building.

The Books

We must keep books and records of our business. This is mandated by the IRS, but more importantly is necessary so we can run our rental property professionally. After all, we need to know and understand how much are we are spending on expenses if we are actually making a profit, how much profit we are making, and how that profit can be maximized.

Our books can be as simple as a handwritten ledger, or as sophisticated as a professional accountant. The trend is to do our own books using software like Quick Books or a spreadsheet. I have used both systems and must admit I am not a big fan of Quick Books. I like to have full control of the numbers. In Quick Books, the calculations are premade and not easy to see what the program is doing. Reports are confusing and hard to tailor to my needs.

I prefer the spreadsheet direction. My setup uses one page per month and I can see everything going on in one screen from amounts past due, current charges to the current outstanding balance. I can also create invoices for all tenants and a profit and loss page, ready to input into my taxes.

I use a Google Spreadsheet that is stored online so I can access the accounting from any computer, even from my smartphone at a rental property. Google Spreadsheet is free. No software to buy or pay for updates.

I have a template of my spreadsheet available for those interested. [rlloyd@clear-lake.com]

Monthly Bookkeeping Template

January 2014 2/7/2014 Tenant	Previous Balance	Current Rent	Utilities	Total Due	~Payments~					Current Balance
					On time	Late 7th~13th	14th~20th	21st plus		
Unit A John Smith	0.00	600		600.00	0	25	-300		-325	0.00
B	0.00			0.00						0.00
C	0.00			0.00						0.00
D	0.00			0.00						0.00
E	0.00			0.00						0.00
F	0.00			0.00						0.00
G	0.00			0.00						0.00
H	0.00			0.00						0.00
I	0.00			0.00						0.00
J	0.00			0.00						0.00
K	0.00			0.00						0.00
L	0.00			0.00						0.00
M	0.00			0.00						0.00
Total	0.00	600.00	0.00	600.00	0.00	25.00	-300.00	0.00	-325.00	0.00

Annual Profit and Loss Statement

Rod Lloyd ~ Property Manager

Rainier Oregon 97048

Phone: 503 _____
Email: _____@clear-lake.com
Webpage: www._____

RENTAL INVOICE

Invoice Date: | 2/21/2014

Due Date | 1st of the month

Tenant: Bill _____
_____
Kelseyville CA 95451

Property Address: _____

DESCRIPTION	AMOUNT
Previous balance	300.00
Recent payments	-300.00
Late charge for last month	
Past Due	0.00
Current Charges:	
Rent 2014 February	300.00

OTHER COMMENTS
1. Late Charge $25 - if not paid in full by the 5th of the month
2. Payment date is the date postmarked if mailed

| | TOTAL Due | 300.00 |

If you have any questions about this invoice, please contact
Rod Lloyd - 503 _____
Make all checks payable to _____

Contact Information	Please report any corrections
Phone home	_____
Phone Cell	_____
email	_____

Taxable Income

One of the many misconceptions of real estate investing is the belief that it is the annual cash flow of a rental property that federal and state incomes taxes are paid on each year. This is quite incorrect.

Annual cash flow and annual income subject to tax are two completely different things. Cash flow may feel like our income since it represents the money we put in our pockets each month but it doesn't take into consideration two very important differences.

To make things clear we should first define cash flow. Cash flow is simply the dollar difference between the checks written and income received each month. If your collected rents for a given month were $1,500 and the checks you wrote for your mortgage payment, property management, utilities, repairs, insurance, etc. totaled $1,200 for the month then you would have had $300 in positive cash flow for that month. Easy enough, but why isn't that also your taxable income?

The first place to look is that mortgage payment. Let's say that out of the $1,200 worth of checks you wrote last month that $900 of it was your mortgage payment. If $800 of your payment was interest and the remaining $100 was repayment of principal then only $800 was truly an expense. The other $100 went towards your equity in the property and can't be counted as an expense on that investment. So now even though we put $300 in cash in our pocket for the month we really had $400 in taxable income. Ouch.

A second place to look would be personal property purchases for the rental. What if one month we purchased a new refrigerator for our rental and it cost $600. Obviously, our cash flow got reduced by $600 [basically we just ate up two months' worth buying the fridge] but did our taxable income also get reduced $600? Unfortunately, no.

When we purchased the refrigerator we traded value. We didn't really have an expense. In essence, we gave the appliance store $600 in value [the $600 in cash] and they, in turn, gave us $600 in value [the $600 fridge]. Our net gain or loss was zero. Only by using the fridge and having time go by does the refrigerator begin to decrease in value. If you think of the fridge being worth $480 a year later due to use then you can see that at that point we laid out $600 a year ago and today the thing we purchased only has $480 in value. Our trade isn't even anymore and we lost [or expensed] $120 in value. This $120 expense is called depreciation.

By now we may be wondering if there is anything that goes the other way and makes our taxable income less than what we received in cash flow. The answer is "yes" and that thing is annual depreciation on the property itself.

Just like our refrigerator example the rental property itself is subject to annual depreciation. Unlike the refrigerator, the property depreciates over 27.5 years instead of five years. For our example let's say the property is worth $150,000 and we can attribute $120,000 of that value to the structure [the house] and the remaining $30,000 to the land [the lot]. In that case, we get to write off as an expense on our property approximately $4,400 [.036 x $120,000] each year. Using our original cash flow example of $300 per month we can see that even though we put $3,600 in our pocket that year [$300 x 12] we actually report an $800 loss for the year! [$3,600 minus $4,400 in depreciation]!

All of this may sound complicated and that is certainly understandable. IRS 1040 Schedule E is really just the document that spells out all of these revenues and expenses for our annual taxes. It's almost like a spreadsheet in its form.

All Cash vs Mortgage Deal

Deal with Financing				Deal All Cash		
Address	344 21st Ave, Longview			Address	344 21st Ave, Longview	
Asking Price	54,900			Asking Price	54,900	
Estimated Sales Price	40,000			Estimated Sales Price	40,000	
Initial Fixup	2,000			Initial Fixup	2,000	
Down payment + Fix-up	25%	12,000		Total Investment		42,000
Loan Amount		10,000				
Interest Rate/2nd 5 yr	3.50%	264.00				
Closing Cost/Total Cash	3,122	15,122				
Mortgage Payment		135.00				
Property Taxes	384	32.00		Property Taxes	384	32.00
Insurance	600	50.00		Insurance	600	50.00
Maintenance [estimated]	19	19.00		Maintenance [estimated]	19	19.00
Utilities	0	0.00		Utilities	0	0.00
Total Expenses		500.00		Total Expenses		101.00
Estimated Rent Income	700	700.00		Estimated Rent Income	700	700.00
NetCashFlow		200.00		NetCashFlow		599.00
Return on Investment		15.87%		Return on Investment		17.11%

If I had written this book a few years ago, I would have said buy as much property as you can with as little money as possible. Up to 2007, leverage was the name of the game. Using other people's money [loans and mortgages] means you have capital appreciation [inflation] on 100% of a property that you pay only a fraction of your own money. Up until 2007 when we bought property, we were 100% sure it would increase in value and not decrease.

I started investing in US real estate in the 80's. Interest rates were in the double-digits. You could buy a property at say $100,000 and in a year or less it was worth $110,000. Even if you overpaid for a property, it would soon catch up and be worth more. That means if you paid $20,000 down payment for the $100,000 property, you made a 50% profit in the first year and it was paid for in two years.

I so miss those years of double-digit interest rates and inflation. It was so easy to make money. Now property prices are not guaranteed to rise, bank interest is just about nothing and there are very few places to invest and get a 5% return without some kind of risk.

If you are just starting out in real estate investing, the hardest deal is the first deal. Unless you have a stash of cash, you will need to scrimp and save just to make a down payment, but it is worth it. I recommend people who want to get started but have little cash, start a two-year savings plan. Cut out BUTTER. By butter, I mean everything that is not ESSENTIAL to life. If it is not housing, food or health, cut it out and save the money. Even the food needs to be rice and beans [as an example], not eating out at restaurants.

Most people, if motivated enough can save enough for a rental property down payment in a manageable amount of time. Stick to your plan and study the real estate market. Go to Zillow.com and you will learn everything you need to know about what property is selling for and renting for in any given neighborhood. Use Zillow to find a rental area that is affordable and determine the typical rental rates for that area. When looking, remember this is not for you to live in, it is to rent out as a BUSINESS.

House For Sale as seen on Zillow

Rentals in the Same Area

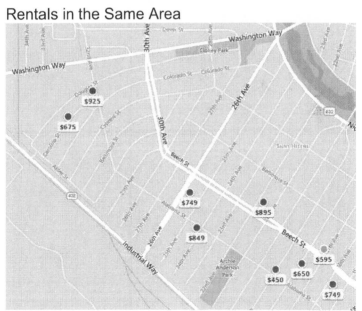

I seem to have gone off on a tangent of getting started in real estate, but this chapter is really about all cash vs mortgage. At this point, I am assuming you are more established or have some investable funds. Investing using mortgages means you can buy more property with less cash. Because you have to cover the loan payments, your net profit will be less. This means you are a high volume, low return investor. With all cash, you are a lower volume, higher return investor. The problem with high volume is you have to deal with a lot of tenants. Tenants, collections, and maintenance will wear you down and there is a danger you will burn out. By paying all cash and having a lower volume, you make more per unit and life is much easier.

Over time, I have transitioned from high volume to low volume and believe my life is so much easier. If there is another real estate crash, it will not bother me. Remember, there are three other ways you make a profit [see chapter above "The Math – How you Make a Profit]

Single Family vs Multi-Family Property

It seems to be assumed that if you are going to own more than one or two rental units, it is better to own an apartment building. The advantages of owning apartment [it is assumed] is it is easier to manage units that are all in one place. Just one roof, not running all over town. These are all good reasons. I want you to consider owning Single Family Dwellings.

Houses Pros

- More desirable / easier to rent
- There are a lot more houses than apartment buildings to pick up bargains
- They are easier to sell when you want to liquidate
- All utilities go in the tenant's name
- More stable tenants [let turnover]
- No grounds or common area to maintain
- Tenants do not gang up against you

Houses Cons

- Tend to be a little more expensive to purchase
- Tend to be more expensive to maintain
- Rentals spread out are harder to manage

Apartment Pros

- Tend to be cheaper per unit to buy
- Less expensive to maintain
- Easier to manage

Apartment Cons

- Exterior is expensive to maintain due to size
- Common areas need upkeep – landscape, trash pickup, lighting, dealing with parking issues
- Complaints from one apartment about another
- Larger buildings need an onsite manager
- Shared utilities paid by the owner [trash, water common area electric]
- Harder to sell

Selecting the Property

The main object of finding the right property is you need the property that returns the most income for your investment. Forget your own taste and preference. It needs to be a good rental area in an affordable rental range. Foreclosures are good. You need to buy at bargain prices. Properties that are not attractive to home buyers, then upgrade the property to rental condition. We do not upgrade to the same standard as house flipping. Tenants will not respect high-end upgrades.

The more bedrooms the better. Single apartments have the highest turnover followed closely by one bedroom units. The three and four bedroom houses attract more stable tenants. The less turnover you have, the more you will make.

Visit all the For Rent homes in the area, keep track of what is attracting higher rents and copy those standards. Clean white walls, neat trim. Clean sanitary bathroom and tidy kitchen.

Utilities

Make sure you understand the utilities. Hopefully, the tenants will be paying most or all the utilities, but this is not always possible. Find out if any of the utility companies in your area put a lien on the property. If the tenant is responsible for paying say the electric bill but they do not pay them and run up a large bill, you will need to pay this bill off when they move out if the electric company puts an automatic lien on the property, in order to transfer it in your name or in the next tenant's name.

Electric

If there is more than one unit, find out if each unit has its own meter. If not, you will have to put the power in your name and somehow figure out how to charge for the electric used by each unit. This is a mess. Sometimes it is possible to have an electrician add sub-meters and you can then accurately bill each tenant, but this might be expensive to set up, and labor-intensive to manage. If tenants are not paying the bill, they will be wasteful with the electric. That is just human nature.

Water

The same is true for water but not as hard to split the bill. Double check the property is on city water. If it has a well, maintaining a well can be expensive. The pump can burn out and cost $1,000 to $2,000 to replace. You would likely have to pay the electric to run the well, adding to your overhead.

Sewer

Like water, make sure it is on city sewer. If the property is on a septic tank, be sure to understand who pumps the tank if it gets full or fails.

I looked at one derelict property. I had a hard time finding out who the owner was. I had a price in my mind that I was willing to pay. It turned out the septic tank had failed and a new system was needed in order to make it habitable. The problem was, it was a small lot and there was not enough room to legally install a new septic system. This property was not purchased. My point is that you need to research carefully before you purchase.

Gas

Again check if city gas is available to the property. All electric homes are more expensive to heat, dry clothes and some people prefer to cook with gas.

Insurance

I believe in having good insurance. It protects your investment and protects you from liability.

If you have put a lot of money into purchasing your rental empire, the last thing you need is to lose it for no fault of your own. Tenants are occupying your property and who knows what they will get up to. They can burn the place down or even blow it up. Next door could catch on fire and jump onto your unsuspecting property. Tenants can get injured or worse and sue what they believe to be a deep pocket. YOU NEED INSURANCE.

When you first buy a property, you have time while it is in escrow. The fact is if you are getting a loan, the mortgage company will require insurance to protect their own interest before they will fund the loan and allow you to close.

One problem you might face is if you are buying a fixer upper, many insurance companies will not cover the place until it is fixed up.... Not good. In that case, you will likely have to pay a high premium to get temporary construction insurance until it is acceptable to the mainstream and more affordable insurance companies.

You do not need contents coverage but you should encourage the tenant to get renters insurance.

It is nice to have one agent to deal with all your properties, but make sure you shop around. You don't want to spend hundreds of dollars more per year just to stick with one company.

Keep a close track of when your renewals are coming due. If you have several properties all with different due dates, it is easy for it to slip by and end up with no insurance. Be professional. Keep on top of it.

Understand what the policy does and does not include. You can often pay a little extra and get loss of income coverage in case the property burns down or whatever and has no income for 6 months or more.

Do not under insure the property. You will be surprised how expensive it is to replace a building. If your property replacement pencils out at $100,000 but you only get $75,000 worth of insurance, you are underinsured and they will only pay 75% of any claim, even if the damage is only $50,000.

Get a high liability limit. If you own lots of assets, others will try everything to get money out of you by any means. One mistake and you could lose everything. Even if you don't make any mistakes, it can be costly to defend yourself from a gold digger.

At this point, some would consider an LLC. It might be a good way to go [in addition to good insurance]. Consult an attorney about this.

Pets & Smoking Rules

Many landlords see pets and smoking as damaging to the unit. I see it the other way, pet owners and smokers will pay more to be allowed to continue their bad habit and to keep their companion. Why limit your market. If you do your own painting and repairs, the damage is easily fixed.

Chances are, even if you say no smoking, there will be smoking going on in the unit. I have rented many units that said no pets in the lease, only to find they soon have a dog, or cat or whatever. They will say they are just looking after it for a friend for a few days. Every time you make a rule, you better be willing to evict them the minute they break the rule or you lose control. I say pick your battles. Don't tell people what they can and cannot do in their own home. They will do it anyway.

Now if you have a high-end condo that might be another story, but I would never rent a high end anyway.

Section 8

Section 8 is a government housing program that assists low-income tenants. If approved, Section 8 pays part of or all of the rent like clockwork. The tenant must be approved by Section 8 and the property must pass inspection. Any defects found during the inspection will need to be corrected prior to the tenant moving in and the rent starting.

Section 8 also makes annual inspections and if it fails inspection, the money stops until corrections are made. This program is not for everyone and adds a level of bureaucracy, but it opens up the rental market to more potential tenants and the money is guaranteed. In the lower value properties, the benefits outweigh the negatives. If you decided to take Section 8, ask them for a written copy of the inspection standards and make sure you follow everything to save delays.

If the tenant breaks any of the terms of the lease, contact the section 8 worker. They should be able to persuade them to behave, or they can be terminated from the section 8 program and lose their rent assistance.

During Escrow

When you are buying your rental, there are lots of things you can do during escrow to save time once escrow closes. The sooner you are ready to rent to tenants, the sooner you start making money.

During the Home Inspection [see House Flipping below] take dozens of pictures, notes, and measurements. Make your plans, design your kitchen and bathroom upgrades; make a list of your general repairs and improvements.

Head over to your home improvement center. Plan on spending some time there and get familiar with what they stock and the prices. Take photos of the items and price. Create a file of all the prices and choices and use these to create your remodeling plan.

Home centers often stock builder quality kitchen cabinets at very reasonable prices. You can buy all the cabinets for $1,000 and up. If they do not have everything in stock, they can get them in a few days. Ask for a price list of all the cabinets. Keep this in your price/materials file and calculate some kitchen designs.

Checkout countertops. They now have some nice laminate tops with a modern edge detail that looks like marble or granite.

Buy some plants and nurture them during escrow at your home so they will be more mature when you finally plant them. Build some inexpensive window boxes ready for closing.

Join your local landlord association. Attend their meetings and glean as much information from them as you can. Get a copy of a standard Rental Agreement or Lease that is legal in your state. Each state has different laws and it is important you use an approved form for your state. You can also ask your realtor if they have a standard lease you can use.

You also need to provide a Mold Guide provided by the EPA and a Lead-Based Paint Guide if older than 1978. I have the tenants sign a document confirming they have received this information and the smoke detector and carbon monoxide detector is working. See the appendix for a copy of this form.

Follow the discussions on The Landlord Protection Agency forum
www.thelpa.com/lpa/forum.html

Go to the website of Bigger Pockets. They have podcasts, articles, networking and training materials on land lording, mostly free
www.biggerpockets.com

Write-up advertising copy. Create a website, ready to use in your advertising. No excuses, there are plenty of no-skill website tools.

Rental Agreement / Lease

Whatever Rental agreement you choose, you should retype it and add some or all of the following clauses.

LATE RENT CHARGES

If Tenant fails to pay the rent in full before the end of the 4th day of the month, Tenant must pay Landlord a late charge as follows: **$5.00 for each day that the rent remains unpaid in full.** Late charges, attorney's fees and any expenses related to the enforcement of this lease shall be classified as "additional rent" or "added rent". Lease violation penalty fees shall be classified as additional rent. This additional rent is payable as rent, together with the next monthly rent due. If the tenant fails to pay additional rent on time, Landlord shall have the same rights against the tenant as if it were a failure to pay rent. The landlord may elect to apply monies received towards past due added rent, paying the oldest charges first.

APPLIANCES

The following appliances are supplied as part of the rental: **Stove & Refrigerator**. Appliances are supplied As-Is, as a convenience and the repair and maintenance of appliances is/are the responsibility of the Tenant.

TENANT BREAKS LEASE

If Tenant breaks this lease, **as liquidated damages**, **the security deposit will be forfeit to the Landlord.**

MOVE OUT CONDITION

Floors must be free of trash and personal items, broom clean. Hard surfaces mopped. Carpets vacuumed and shampooed. Windows washed. Kitchen clean especially the stove. All cupboards and draws empty and wiped out. Bathroom clean especially the toilet. If the paint was new on move-in, it is expected to be serviceable for at least 2 years. If the tenancy is less than 2 years and needs repainting, a prorated charge will be made. Daily rent will be charged for the reasonable time it takes to make repairs.

FINAL INSPECTION (AFTER MOVE OUT)

A) Landlord will inspect the unit immediately **after** the tenant has moved out.
B) If the Landlord finds any damages, they will be listed on a final inspection sheet and deducted from the security deposit, [labor at $25/hr plus materials]. A security deposit refund/accounting will be mailed to Tenant's new address no later than 14 days from Landlord's receiving possession of the unit and received the keys.
C) Tenant will be responsible for damages that exceed the security deposit.

EMERGENCY CONDITIONS

In the event the unit becomes unhabitable in the Landlords opinion, the rent may be suspended for the immediate duration of the condition [major water or sewer leak, major roof leak, major structural failure, major electrical problem etc]. Landlord's maximum obligation to the tenant is $25 per day for alternative living expenses.

Close of Escrow

The day escrow closes is the day your work kicks into high gear. Plan on working full time until the unit is ready to rent.

On day one, cut the grass, edge and power wash the front. Start greening up the lawn by watering every day if necessary. You can set up a temporary automatic watering system if needed. Add fertilizer and over-seed the lawn. Hang some hanging baskets.

Tidy up small details that will improve the curb appeal AND put out the For Rent sign. You never know, someone might come the first day and rent the unit, subject to you fixing the major problems. At this point, you do not need to promise too much, see where the conversation goes. You do need to upgrade anything unsafe or unsanitary, but other than that, if they are happy with the cosmetic side, run with the deal.

Turn on your marketing. Place an ad on Craig's List. Turn on your website vacancy page. Use lots of photos, even add a floorplan.

Upgrades

Assuming you do not get a quick bite, start your work in earnest. Start with the front exterior curb appeal, and then work on the living room, kitchen and main bathroom in that order. These are the priority items to lookers. Tell interested tenants the rest of the house will be completed to the same standard and they will work with you.

Occasionally you will get a tenant that is so eager to move-in, they will agree to finish the work for a discount in the security deposit. I would not accept such an offer and they almost never finish the work and could file a claim that the place is unsafe, and they would likely win.

A couple of things I always do at the very start of the project is:

Let off a Bomb – a bug bomb to be precise. You never know what is letting in the cracks and crevices. Bugs, even bug eggs waiting for the right conditions to come to haunt you. Once a tenant moves in, if they report bugs, you better take it seriously. The health department of eviction judge will nail YOU to correct the problem. A professional exterminator will cost hundreds of dollars. One bug bomb costing less than $2 can potentially save all that.

Liquid Draino – is the second item. You don't know what the last occupant put down the drain or when the last time the drains were cleaned. Simply putting a good glug of drain-opening liquid down each drain and save a lot of grief. The thicker the liquid the better.

Safety Upgrades

Buildings are built [hopefully] to the current building codes. Codes seem to be a bureaucratic nuisance, but it is for everyone's benefit and safety in the long run. I have been lucky enough to visit many countries in my life and seen firsthand what happened when strong building codes are not in place or enforced.

Codes are updated every few years, based on statistical data from accidents and reports from disasters.

Buildings constructed in the 50's 60's and even 70's are often not up to current code. There is usually no requirement to upgrade a building to current codes unless you plan on making a big alteration to the original building or use, or after a fire or other major damage.

Buildings also become functionally obsolescent, meaning it is out of date, such as modern open plan floor layout and kitchens more suited to entertaining. Bathrooms can also become dated and less attractive when it comes to renting a vacancy. The trick is only to upgrade what will bring in the most net profit. You are not updating to your taste, don't fall in love with your property, make sound business decisions based on the people likely to rent your property, decisions that will make it easy to rent and easy to maintain, while bringing in a good income.

However, there are some important items to focus on.

- The electrical system must be safe and be able to supply enough power to meet the demands of your tenants. The last thing you want is power strips all over the place and overloaded circuits.
- All stairs and changes in elevation must have handrails for the convenience and safety of your tenants and protection for your liability.
- Walkways and stairs must be free from tripping hazards and well lighted. There are endless attorneys all ready to work for your tenants on a commission basis for a trip and fall lawsuit.
- Peeling paint is a big turn off for potential tenants and maybe a lead paint hazard.
- The windows must work, not only for ventilation but to act as fire escapes in the event of an emergency. This is often a good time to upgrade to modern vinyl thermal windows that are easy to operate and more efficient.
- Window locks must be operable, especially if close to the ground.
- Smoke detectors are mandatory and often carbon monoxide detectors also.

What not to Include

It might sound counterproductive, but everything you include in your rental, you are obligated to maintain. In the economy rental market, tenants just want a clean safe home, and extras will generally not help you rent it or get you any more money. Believe me.

The following items, if installed in your rental should be **removed** at the first opportunity [when it is next vacant and before any tenants look at the property]

- Dishwasher
- Garbage Disposal
- Door Bell
- Door and Window Screens [unless mandated by your state]
- Storm windows
- Stove
- Refrigerator
- Washer and Dryer
- Laundry hookups if you are paying for the water
- Window treatments
- Ceiling Fans
- Garage Door Opener
- Exterior hose bibs [faucets] if you are paying for the water

- Adjust the Water Heater temperature down, especially electric units, if you are paying the electric bill
- Security system
- Air Conditioner
- Trash Compactor
- Sink sprayer or soap dispenser
- Any other non-essential appliances, fixtures or fittings

Marketing

There is no one way to find tenants, you need to follow all avenues.

The first and most obvious is the for rent sign in the front window or yard. If it is a popular rental area, this will often be all that is needed. It might also attract vandals to break in and cause damage and steal any tools and materials you have inside.

Craigslist is free and should also be the next choice. Include lots of information, photos, a floor plan and your contact information.

There are also many online rental services in your neighborhood that allow free listings like Zillow.com and Trulia.com.

If the unit is not moving, the next level is newspaper advertising. This can be expensive, but having a vacant unit for an extra month is even more expensive.

Also try notices on the local bulletin boards at grocery stores, post office, Section 8 office etc.

If you have web skills, create a website for your rentals and use the web address in your ads so people can get more information about your vacancy. It can include all the details, photos, information about the schools and community, your forms etc. Often you can find a friend or high school student that will do the web page for you.

The time of year might affect response. It is very hard to rent a unit near Christmas. Summer is the best time. I write my lease so they all end on June 30th no matter when they move in. If they renew that is fine, if they decide to move on at the end of the lease, it is the best time to get it re-rented.

I choose to have a separate phone number to use for my rental business. I use Google Voice. It will provide a free local number that is very customizable. You can have it send the calls to an existing landline or cell phone number or both. It can have a different ringtone and if you do not answer, it allows them to leave a message that it transcribes to text and can send you an email of the message. I like it because I never miss a call, especially important if I am advertising a vacant unit and am working in the unit. I can tell them to come on over.

I have also used a PO Box to have rents sent to so I do not get unwanted visitors to my home.

I never admit to being the owner of the property. I tell them I am the Manager. When confronted with tricky requests that are hard to say no to face to face, I tell them I have to ask the owner and after reflection tell them the owner's decision. This way I can stay the tenant's friend and let the owner get the blame for hard decisions. [*Can I have a Pit Bull? Sorry, the owner said NO*]

Discrimination

You might be tempted to skip this section but I strongly recommend you read it very carefully and follow the principals. Even if you are the most moral and ethical person in the world, if you don't take precautions, you can end up having to defend your decisions at huge expense and I mean up to $100,000.

Now that I have your attention, to state the obvious, you are not allowed to discriminate against **protected classes**:

- Race – Civil Rights Act of 1964
- Color – Civil Rights Act of 1964
- Religion – Civil Rights Act of 1964
- National origin – Civil Rights Act of 1964
- Age (40 and over) – Age Discrimination in Employment Act of 1967
- Sex – Equal Pay Act of 1963 and Civil Rights Act of 1964
- Pregnancy – Pregnancy Discrimination Act
- Citizenship – Immigration Reform and Control Act
- Familial status – Civil Rights Act of 1968 Title VIII: Housing cannot discriminate for having children, with an exception for senior housing
- Disability status – Vocational Rehabilitation and Other Rehabilitation Services of 1973 and Americans with Disabilities Act of 1990

- Veteran status – Vietnam Era Veterans' Readjustment Assistance Act of 1974 and Uniformed Services Employment and Reemployment Rights Act
- Genetic information – Genetic Information Nondiscrimination Act
- Others might also apply in your state or jurisdiction.

It is very important that you have a system in place, in case you are challenged, to show how you arrived at approving some people and rejecting others. It is not adequate to just use your personal judgment and gut feeling. If you create a standard policy for accepting tenants and follow it, you are a long way to protecting yourself if someone feels the world owes them the right to a place to stay no matter what, especially if they know how to use the system.

Some look for sloppy managers to create a nuisance complaint. You will need to hire a lawyer to defend yourself and likely you will pay a nuisance settlement.

The local housing authority has people called 'testers' whose job it is to call rental listings, throw out some statements that might tempt you to turn them down, then zap, you are busted. They may have two callers contact you on different days with different stories to see how welcoming you are. They might say things like 'they use medical marijuana', or 'have a comfort animal', or they 'need wheelchair access'. I recommend that you include on your application, the question: Are you a tester? A tester MUST answer truthfully!

The best policy is to be welcoming to everyone calling you and invite them to see the unit. Allow them to fill out an application and see where that takes you.

Suggested Rental Policy

- Your gross income must equal approximately three times the monthly rent of your home.
- A favorable credit history.
- Be employed or be able to furnish acceptable proof of the required income.
- Good references from previous Landlords.
- Applicant must have all the move-in money available.
- Applicant must be over 18 years old.

Only reject an applicant based on one of the items on your policy. Note some are arbitrary like "A favorable credit history" or "Good references from previous Landlords"

Always display the Equal Housing logo in your marketing material [and follow the rules].

EQUAL HOUSING
OPPORTUNITY

YOU are already a protected class. Look back at the list and see what might apply to you.

Safe Advertising

Make sure you don't violate the discrimination rules in your advertising. The rule is 'describe the property, not the people'.

An example of good phrases

Three bedrooms

An example of a bad phrases

Suitable for a family

Do you think it acceptable to say a rental is near a school or a church? I invite you to do your own research on that to further your knowledge on this subject.

Painting

It is my long experience that by far the biggest job for the landlord is painting. In a typical two-week remodel of a vacant unit, I will spend more than ½ the time painting. This is, of course, a generalization, but most of the time it seems to hold true.

Remember I worked for a company that had 462 units, employed 4 painters, 1 carpenter, 1 plumber/electrician and 1 handyman. Note the ratio of work.

Most tenants are hard on a property. If I paint a room at my home, it is likely to look good for ten years or more. Not so with a rental. I had one rental that had fresh paint when the tenant moved in, and when evicted 10 weeks later, needed a complete two-coat paint job, mainly because lots of kids were left unattended, crayoning on the walls, dirty hand marks, lipstick on the ceilings, grease in the kitchen. While this is the exception, it does illustrate the point, paint is big!

To be fair, I have also had units with still great paint after a one-year rental. In general, I budget for giving a unit a two-coat paint job every two years [only when vacant].

First let's talk about what type of paint to use. Paint is not cheap when you consider how much you can go through in a year. On the other hand, it is a job you can do yourself, or even pay low-skilled workers to paint for you [with close supervision].

The traditional basic paint job uses two types of paint. Flat for the living space and semi-gloss for the kitchen and bathroom. This plan is not ideal for a rental. The main problem with flat paint is it seems to absorb dirt – handprints and the like. The advantage is it is the cheapest and easiest to apply.

Many landlords use semi-glass throughout the unit. Semi-glass is washable [to some degree] but it is more expensive and shows every defect in the wall surface. I hate the look of semi-gloss paint.

I have settled on middle ground – eggshell. Eggshell can be used in all areas including kitchens and bathrooms, does not absorb the dirt and is cheaper and easier to apply. Also, I only have to buy one product which is very convenient.

Long ago, I made the decision to paint the interior of all my rentals the same color for efficiency. I chose cream. Cream is neutral and softer than white but very warm and cheerful. I paint everything cream – walls, trim, baseboards, and ceilings. If any unit becomes vacant or need a touch up after a repair, out comes the cream and it quickly blends in with the rest of the unit. I buy it by the 5-gallon bucket.

What is the Best Paint?

There has been endless discussion about the various types of paint. Many swear by the brand they have been using for years, be it Sherwin Williams [Property Solution], Lowes [Valspar], Home Depot [BEHR] or whatever. I was never impressed with the bragging because they never do a comparison.

I decided to do my own comparison. I had a three-bedroom unit to paint so I bought paint for each of the three mentioned above [mainly because they are all local for me]. Each covered about the same and each looked the same at the end of the day. My conclusion is they are comparable.

I settled on the Property Solution from Sherwin Williams, but the first thing you need to know about Sherwin Williams is they play price games. The retail price for Property Solution is approaching $200 for 5 gallons but if you open an account as a property manager, you can get big discounts. I pay under $100 for 5 gallons. I am very happy with that.

I have since moved to Home Depots Behr Pro [PR170]. I can shop for all my supplies while they mix up my paint, and it's ready to go out the door when I am.

One more thing to note, you should only buy latex paint, which is water based, not oil based. Oil-based paints are a beast to clean up, especially your rollers and brushes. Latex paint cleans up under running water.

Preparation

Prep is everything. If you do not do proper prep, you might be wasting your time and paint.

- Remove all furniture, personal items, and trash from the room.
- Sweep away Cobwebs, wipe down any dust and dirt on the old paint.
- Remove nails etc. from the walls and woodwork.

- Fill the holes left from nail holes etc. [see drywall chapter].
- Remove electrical plates from the outlets and switches [keep them safe]
- Remove door latches and keeper plates.
- Remove other fixtures – heater covers, curtain rails, ceiling fan blades etc. etc.

How to apply the paint

- I have tried everything, rollers, pads and sprayers and keep going back to rollers. I start with the extra wide rollers, 18" wide with ¾" nap. The nap is how fat the roller is. The fatter the roller, the more paint it holds. The more paint on your roller, the faster the job goes, which is very important. The fatter nap also fills imperfections in the wall better and leaves a little-mottled effect on the wall which can disguise imperfections in the wall finish.

The 18" roller frame is much stronger than the flimsy 9" roller frames. You will need a bigger roller tray for this setup.

- For smaller rooms I use the standard 9" rollers and upgrade to a 1 ¼" nap, and for tight spaces and touch up, I drop down to a 4" roller. Actually, they only seem to have these shorter rollers in a very fine nap, so I cut a 9" roller in half with a hacksaw and end up with two small rollers with a fat nap.

- I do 90% of my painting with this setup, using a cut-in brush for hitting where the rollers miss [in the corners and at edges]. Also, I **roll first** and **cut in second**. I find this much faster than cutting in first then rolling second because you know what needs to be hit and the fresh paint on the wall from the roller spreads into the corners without adding much paint to the brush.

- I use an adjustable roller pole. When I first tried this pole, I was amazed how useful it was. It quickly adjusts from 3' up to 6' so getting in tight spaces I use it short and extend it when rolling the ceiling. They also make longer adjustable roller poles for the exterior.

- When rolling, DO NOT paint over the electric outlets and switches. Roll as close as you can then cut in with a brush.

Dropcloths

It is important to use drop cloths when painting, even if you plan to replace the flooring, it is still best to protect everything.

They make plastic, disposable drop cloths. Don't even think of using anything plastic, including tarps.

When paint lands on plastic, it sits there for a long time, just waiting for you to step on it and tread it all around, even beyond the drop cloth. While we are at it, don't use old bed sheets or newspaper. Yes, they will absorb the drops of paint, but it will soak through and deposit the paint on whatever it is sitting on.

Instead, invest in about three canvas drop cloths. A very large one, room size [say 10' by 12']. A smaller one, for smaller rooms [say 6' by 8'] and a runner, [say 3' by 8'] for when you are painting single walls.

MDF Strips

One of my own inventions is homemade mdf strips. I take a 2' by 4' by 1/8" mdf [medium density

fiberboard, available at the home store] and cut it in half to make two 1' by 4'. I have several sets of these and they are handy to protect a floor or countertop etc. when making small paint jobs and touch-ups. Some I cut profiles to fit standard doorways and jambs. I can cut in baseboard and paint doors and door jambs without having to drag out the drop cloths and you can get right down to the floor. Create some shorter strips for tight spaces [1', 2' & 3']. Make sure you store them flat. They are no good if they have a bend to them. Note- mine only have the cream paint on them.

Paint Cup

When you are cutting in, pour an inch or two into a paint cup [never more than two inches of paint or it will get all over the handle]. This makes the cutting in go much faster. This one even has a magnetic brush holder to store the brush out of the paint for short periods.

Loading your Brush

One of the biggest mistakes people make is incorrectly loading a brush. By loading, I mean putting the correct amount of paint on [actually in] the brush. A typical

brush has hairs about 1 ½" long. Most of the time you should only be dipping the brush ½" into the paint. If you are getting paint on the metal part of the brush, you are overloading the brush and your job will suffer. Once you have dipped the brush into the paint ½", tap the hairs on the **side** [inside] of the paint can or cup, to set the paint into the hairs and remove excess. DO NOT scrape the hair on the rim of the can, this just takes the paint off the brush again.

When cutting in, I only dip ¼" into the paint to create a controllable bead as I draw the brush.

Second Coat

So many times I see someone's paint job that obviously needed a second coat. I always plan on painting two coats. The second coat is very quick to apply [compared to the first coat] and makes the job look twice as nice. I consider it a bonus if a second coat is not needed.

Impossible Wall Stains

From time to time, you will find marks on the wall from things like crayon, marker, spray paint or who know what else. These marks will bleed through the paint, even after 5 coats. On your first walk through the unit, make note of such marks and apply a stain blocker a day before you start full-on painting. I use Kilz water based Stain blocker available at Home Depot. A quart will be plenty for lots of stains and will make your paint job go much better.

Caulking

Nothing finishes off a paint job like caulking. Gaps between the molding and a wall bug me and make a job look sloppy. Buy a box of painter's caulk. It is cheap and if you have it handy, you will likely use it.

The fact is, you can do some caulking with paint. Whenever you see a small gap between

 molding [baseboard or door trim whatever] add a little extra paint to the brush and hit the joint. Often that will be enough to fill the gap. Use caulk for the larger gaps. Use you damp finger to create a nice bead. Give the caulk a day to set up a little and touch up with paint.

 Caulk is needed around countertops and around the tub/shower. Remove any old nasty looking grout first.

Front Door

The one exception to my cream color scheme is the front door. I like to paint the outside of the front door a strong red. It sets the house off nicely and makes a good first impression.

Cleanup

Make sure you wash out the brushes and rollers as soon as you are finished with them. Take the roller cover off the roller or they will get stuck on to the roller frame. Properly cleaned and stored, they will last a very long time.

Drywall

It is surprisingly common to find holes in walls. The most common place is behind the door from the doorknob, but I have found holes all over the place.

Holes in walls tend to freak people out. It certainly is a sign of outrageous conduct on the part of the tenant. Personally, holes in the walls are no big deal to me because I know how easy and cheap they are to fix, but it looks good as a defense to keep a security deposit. Holes also drive down the price of vacant homes so I can pick them up for a song.

Start by cutting a square of drywall a little bigger than the damage.

Draw around the drywall square onto the wall and cut out the hole with a jab saw.

Place an offcut of wood inside the wall, screwed through from the front.

Insert the drywall patch and screw in place.

The next step is to apply drywall compound.

Drywall compound is very easy to work with if you know the tricks.

The first thing to know is drywall compound when fully set can be sanded very easily to make it flat. The problem with sanding drywall mud is it creates a very fine dust that gets everywhere. Believe me, it makes a mess in the whole house.

Soon after getting married, I was remodeling the entry hall of our home. I needed to add some drywall and tape the joints. This was my first attempt at anything more than a small patch. I laid the compound on thick, knowing I could sanding it flat when it dried. I used my power sander to wack it down and when I stepped back to admire my work, I was very proud. A few minutes later Merry came home from work. She freaked out. It was like it snowed in the house. Everything had a white coating, even in the master bedroom and closet. It took her a week to get it cleaned up. Luckily, making up is fun when newly married.

There is a better way.

The trick is to apply the mud in layers. The first layer is just intended to fill in the gaps and NOT protrude past the wall surface. The first layer can

take up to two or three days to fully set, depending on how thick you make it and the temperature/humidity. Add drywall mesh over bigger gaps. When it is fully set, use a wider blade to make a micro-thin next coat, still making sure it does not protrude from the wall surface. This layer will only take a few hours to dry because it was so thin. Continue adding layers until it is completely flat and level with the wall surface. It might take three, four or even five layers. Just make sure they are micro thin, filling the depressions each time.

Each layer only takes a minute to apply so the total time over several days only adds up to a few minutes. To be the most productive, scour the complete rental and work all holes and defects at the same time. Fill nail holes and divets. If you find lumps on the wall, use a hammer and gently tap the hole to make a slight dent. The purpose is to push all the drywall back in towards the wall, because removing whatever was stuck in the wall normally pulls the drywall out. This creates a little divot which can then be filled in with joint compound and smoothed flat.

Drywall compound comes in three flavors:

- All Purpose
- Topping
- Fast Set

I buy the Topping because it ends up with a smoother finish. It comes in a box or in a bucket. The bucket is much more expensive. Buy the box [under $10] and transfer some to a sealable Tupperware container. Always keep it sealed. Drywall compound is very similar to spackling and the like but is easier to work with and much, much cheaper.

For larger holes, you can and should use Fast Set. It comes in a powder and needs to be mixed with water. It comes in different setting times 20, 45, 90 minutes etc. These numbers represent the drying time. I recommend the longer set times. You will be able to start applying the finishing coats the same day.

The Ultimate Door Stop

As shown above, the door handle can cause a lot of damage by the careless tenant. There are lots of door stops on the market.

This spring kind is cheap and very popular but tends

to be irresistible to kids, the twang it makes when kicked. Sooner or later they get bent over or broken off. Soon after a hole appears in the wall.

This one fits on the hinge. It puts a lot of stress on the hinge and will likely pry the door screws out of the frame.

You can add a bumper or protective plate on the wall where the doorknob will hit, but this will not stand up to the more aggressive tenants.

I create my own. I cut a 2" x 4" into 4" blocks and screw them to the floor with long screws. That fixes the problem for good at very little cost. Paint them the same color as your walls.

Plumbing

This is likely to be one of those subjects you will be tempted to say, this I cannot or will not do.

With a little study, you will find plumbing repairs amongst the easiest in the rental business. A typical repair takes 30 minutes and needs just a little common sense. Making your own plumbing repairs will save you hundreds of dollars.

Most of the problems fall under these headings:

- Toilets
- Faucets
- Drains

Let's jump right in, the water is fine.

I recently had hip surgery. Needless to say, I could not do my own repairs for a few weeks after my surgery. Wouldn't you know it, I had two plumbing problems come up the week after my surgery, both on the same day. One was a bathtub drain leaking in an upstairs apartment onto a bed in the downstairs apartment. It cost me over $400 for Mr. Rooter to replace the tub drain.

The second was a leaking water supply pipe under the kitchen sink [in a different rental]. Another $400. It took all day to beg the plumber to come out, wait for arrival and then get him to go to the next problem. I could have done both in an hour but it served as a reminder how much I save by doing my own work.

Toilets

A standard toilet consists of two basic mechanisms, one to fill the tank and a second to flush the bowl. You don't need any tools to pop off the toilet tank lid to see how it works and make adjustments. Just be careful, the lid is likely porcelain and brittle. It will break if dropped and they are hard to replace. I set it in the tub or shower out of the way.

On the left side is the flexible water supply line coming from the angle stop [shut off valve at the wall]. That connects to a threaded fitting at the bottom left of the tank. This is often just hand tight. The threaded fitting is the bottom of the filler valve. This valve only allows water to enter when the water level is low [after a flush]. It has a float valve that shuts the water off when it reaches a set level. This level is easily adjustable. Watch some YouTube videos on toilet filler valve and look at the toilets in your house.

The flush valve is usually a rubber flapper that seals the large opening to the toilet bowl. A chain connects to the flush handle. It has an air pocket that keeps the flapper open when activated until all the water has descended to the bowel.

Common Toilet Problems

The first problem might be a leaking supply pipe. Turn off the angle stop valve, screw off the pipe at both ends, take the pipe to the plumbing store and get a replacement.

Another problem is a "running toilet", meaning it is constantly filling. This could be one of two faults.

The ball valve might have failed, if so remove the ball valve, take it to the plumbing store and get a replacement. [see YouTube for procedure]

It might just need adjusting, to lower the water level to just below the overflow tube.

Or it might need the flapper replacing. Turn off the water, pop off the flapper from its hooks and disconnect the chain. Install a new flapper.

Once you understand toilets, it is best to have in stock a kit

- one water supply pipe,
- one modern ball valve
- one flapper

One last problem, the flush handle may be broken or not flushing correctly.

If it is broken, unscrew the lock nut on the inside of the tank [which usually has a left-hand thread], disconnect the chain and install a replacement.

If it is not broken but not flushing correctly, make sure the chain is connected or adjust the chain to another link setting, and retest until working.

Faucets

The kitchen and bathroom faucets get a lot of use and abuse. The common problems are:

- Leaks
- Broken Faucet

Faucet Leaks

The older style of faucet has a screw that closes the water flow by pressing a rubber washer against a metal seat. The rubber washer tends to wear out quite quickly and can be replaced. Sometimes the seat itself gets damaged. The seat also can be replaced.

 More modern faucets use a cartridge that lasts much longer and is easier to replace than the washer and seat.

A third option is to just replace the faucet when it shows the first sign of problems. Some choose to replace with a substantial faucet [say over $50] and change the stems when they cause a little trouble [leaks]. My preference is to replace the faucet with the least expensive faucet [under $20]. It is a little more trouble but looks nicer and you tend to get about 5 years of trouble free use out of a new faucet.

To replace a faucet, turn off the water at the angle stop valve. Disconnect the water pipe [hose] at the bottom of the faucet. You might needs a basin wrench for that [a specially made wrench for just this job]. Next undo the lock nuts from under the counter and the faucet will come off.

Washer

Hose

Valve

Flexible tube

Stub-out

Basin wrench

Shutoff valve

Clean off the counter where the old faucet sat. Add some caulk on the underside of the new faucet and reverse the steps.

It should only take 20 or 30 minutes to do this job and could save a late night emergency call down the road.

Tub/Shower Faucet

Shower valves are a little – well a lot different. First of all you do not have a convenient shut-off valve nearby so you will have to turn the water off at the main.

Once the water is off, your only inexpensive choice is to repair the washer/seat if it is an older faucet or replace the cartridge if it is a newer unit. Replacing the complete valve means tearing open the walls etc.

Dismantle the faucet stem slowly and carefully, noting where everything came from (Pictures with your cell phone can be helpful in a case like this). Put a towel over the drain so you don't lose any small parts down the plug hole.

Take the stem to the plumbing store and get the necessary parts [either a replacement washer or a complete new stem] and reinstall. Note: DO NOT start a project like this when the local store is closed. You need plenty of time so things go smoothly. Deadlines are deadly.

Drain Leaks

I can't count how many times I have seen drain pipes with all kinds of supposed waterproof compounds, trying to stop a water leak.

Drain assemblies are quite simple to understand and make watertight if you know how they work. It is actually more difficult to use these compound fixes than doing it right. I am not saying I would not consider using a goop, if it was midnight and I had guests over, but a goop fix is always temporary and you are just delaying when the next leak will pop up.

Firstly there are two types of drain – metal and plastic. Each is fine. There is nothing wrong with the inexpensive white plastic drain pipe systems. Leave the fancy chrome fittings to exposed locations like public restrooms and hotel rooms.

It seems like no two drain setups are alike, but the concept is always the same. The sink comes down, incorporates a 'trap' and ends up entering the building drainage system at the wall [or floor]. Sometimes two sinks connect together making it look more complicated.

We are not going to discuss how to design these systems. All you need to know is how to dismantle an existing system, replace any defective parts and put it back together again so it does not leak and will not leak causing an emergency call from your tenant.

The secret to this joint is the tailpiece washer and you are advised to have some spares ready for repairs.

This is called a Slip Joint. Note the nylon ring that creates the watertight seal. If this ring gets damaged, they are inexpensive and readily available, so it is good to have several on hand for repairs.

With a couple of simple parts in stock and a pair of large channel lock pliers, making drain repairs are very simple.

12" Channel Lock Pliers

Electrical

Again, electrical might me your nightmare repair. Fact; a healthy respect for electric is good! I will run you through the most common and not complicated repairs that we are faced with:

- Outlets
- Switches
- Light fixtures

These repairs are very straightforward

Some Electrical Tools you Need

I am going to recommend a couple of simple tools to buy. They are valuable to the landlord even if you do not plan to do your own electrical work.

 An outlet tester will tell you if an outlet is working if it is wired correctly and if a GFCI outlet is wired and working correctly [more on GFCI later]. This is good when you are considering buying a property, and checking it between tenants.

A non-contact electrical tester will tell you if there is power to an item, be it a switch, outlet or wire, without having to touch the live wire or terminal itself. It can save you getting a shock when you think the power is off, or tell you if a wire is live.

Replacing an Electrical Outlet

Assuming you can turn the power off to the offending outlet, it is very safe to replace an existing defective outlet. I do recommend turning off the power to the whole house if you are nervous about working with electric but I will leave that up to you after you have read this section.

Assuming an outlet is broken or caked with paint, follow this procedure.

- Remove the cover plate, one small screw in the center of the plate. Set the plate and screw aside.
- Unscrew the two screws top and bottom of the outlet. The new outlet will include new screws.

- Pull the outlet out of the box. It will have about 6" of extra wire to allow you to disconnect the wires from the terminals. As you disconnect each wire, keep track of where it was connected so you can re-connect them the same way to the new outlet. You can make a diagram if you like, or put tags on each wire. The bottom line is the white wires connect to the silver colored side of the new outlet, and the black wires connect to the brass colored side. The green or bare wire connects to the green terminal at the bottom of the new outlet.
- Push the new outlet and extra wires back into the box and screw it in place.
- Reinstall the cover plate, turn on the power and test with your outlet tester to make sure it is all correct.

When you try to install the cover plate, you might find it does not sit flush with the wall. The outlet might be too far out or recessed too far in. Do not over tighten the screw to the cover plate. The plate is brittle and will crack. If the plate does not sit right, adjust the top and bottom screws to the outlet until the plate will sit flush with the wall.

Just a note about the number of wire's you might encounter inside the box. You might find it has one of each wire [black, white and bare] or two sets. Just connect the wires to the new outlet like it was connected to the old outlet.

If you encounter burned or otherwise damaged wires, contact a licensed electrical contractor!!

Replacing a Light Switch

 The procedure for a light switch is very similar to replacing an outlet. Just replace the wires to the new switch like they came off the old switch. Any wires in the box that are connected together with a wire nut, just leave alone, do not disconnect the wire nut.

If you need to replace a three-way switch [where two switches operate one light], make sure you buy a new three-way switch and replace the wires as they came off the old switch.

Replacing a light fixture

Replacing an old light fixture with a new modern fixture is a great way to upgrade a unit. Again, connect the new fixture just the same way the old fixture was connected.

Floors

As mentioned previously, I do not do carpeting. I have tried it and made a half-way decent job, but I have never been happy with my own carpeting job. Besides, carpets and tenants do not match. It is very disheartening to have new or perfectly good carpet destroyed by a careless

tenant.

I like to install laminate flooring. I think it looks nicer, is easy to keep clean and is less likely to be damaged by a tenant. I can install a laminate floor in a bedroom in about 3 hours.

Installing Laminate Flooring

Laminate flooring comes in various qualities and prices. For a rental, I would not put anything down but the cheapest variety. I am paying 69 cents per sq ft at Home Depot. They keep it separate from most of the flooring, hoping you will not find it. Hunt it down. Do not trust they will have more of the same if you run out. Read the box for how many sq ft a box covers, measure your room carefully. Buy one extra box and take it back if you do not use it [keep the receipt].

Deliver the flooring to your unit and leave for a day or two before installing. The laminate floor does not need any more than that because it is a very stable product. I do not use any underlayment. I have never had a problem having installed dozens of floors.

You will need to buy a couple of special tools and make one homemade jig.

Buy a tapping block and a pull bar

Next, make a homemade cutting jig. This is not mandatory but without the jig, you will be getting up and down off your knees dozens of time without it and at my age, that would be a deal breaker.

Other tools you will need are

- Hammer
- Kneeling Pad
- Battery saw
- Pencil

Kitchen and Bathroom Floors

In the kitchen and bathroom, vinyl is better to install but you must get a good quality vinyl. The thin stuff will tear before you get it down and will not hold up to tenant abuse. Another option is peel & stick tiles. They are even easier to work with but your subfloor must be in good condition. If it is not, you will need to add a new 3/8" plywood subfloor.

Doors and Locks

Solid Core doors are a must. Hollow core doors are a magnet for holes and abuse.

Locks

Assuming you own more than a couple of rental units, you are now in the lock business. When you first buy your rental property, it is strongly advised you change the locks because you have no idea who might still have keys to these locks and therefore access to your rental unit.

Now, these old locks are likely perfectly good locks, at least in working order, and you have the keys, so it makes no sense to throw these locks away because you will be changing locks a lot in the future.

Assuming you own other rental units, you are likely to have spare locks in storage, so you can install one of these on your new rental.

When you find a tenant for your rental, you will need to hand over a couple of keys to each of the locks. You also need to keep a copy of all the keys for emergencies. So you will need to visit a locksmith or hardware store to get more keys made. Better get some key tags while you are at it and mark the keys you keep. Better still buy or make a simple key rack with a place for keys for each of your rental units. You can easily make a rack with an offcut of wood or plywood and some cup hooks.

Be sure to store the keys somewhere safe.

You are now in a never-ending cycle of lock changes. You never know when you are going to need a lock. Lock prices can range from $11 to over $100. There is nothing wrong with the $11 variety. You can often find them at yard sales. Ideally, you should have all your locks the same make.

Kwikset

I always use Kwikset locks. There are several reasons why, and no I do not have stock in Kwikset.

Firstly, they are the most common locks, at least in my area.

Secondly, they are inexpensive.

Thirdly, they are easy to rekey and we will get into that later.

Having all your locks the same make, you can interchange parts as needed. There is nothing wrong with using a different make of locks if that works for you.

SIDENOTE

At the same time as running rental properties, I owned a restaurant business. I decided for the business to use Schlage locks because someone told me they were safer.

One day I was in conversation with a customer when business was slow. She was a locksmith and when I mentioned I used Schlage locks on the business because I believed them to be safer, she headed for the door and asked me to lock her out. I complied and within 15 seconds she opened the door with a pick. She assured me most locks can easily be picked with a little practice.

This brings up the subject of security. As a landlord, we are obligated to provide reasonable security. Kwikset locks provide Reasonable security, so why pay more?

Deadbolts

Some jurisdictions require a deadbolt on all exterior doors, while others do not. Also, insurance or rental assistance programs may also require deadbolts. It definitely adds to the security to some degree but also adds cost to the landlord.

The advantage of adding a deadbolt, besides having a second locking mechanism, the deadbolt design has a much stronger bolt, 1" long of hardened steel.

Before you go off on the security thing, remember your rental has glass windows and at some point, added locks are just wasted. If someone wants to get in, they will find a way and the more obstacles you put in the way, the more damage they will cause.

Double Deadbolts are deadbolt locks that require a key on both the outside and inside. People often use them when there is glass in the door or next to the door. **They are illegal** for residential use because someone could be trapped inside during a fire and unable to escape. Adding one of these locks in a rental will endanger your tenants and expose you to a big liability.

Rekeying Locks

From time to time you will end up with locks that have no key, or you might want to make all the locks in a unit [or your own home] have the same key. You can even master-key all your rentals if you know how to rekey locks.

It would be tricky to fully describe how to rekey a Kwikset lock in this document. I recommend you go on YouTube and do a search. Watch several and see how easy it is. You can rekey a lock quicker than it takes to have one cut at the hardware store and save a lot of money. You will need to buy a kit but saving one or two locks with no key will pay for itself. It will include a few very simple tools, pins and the instructions. It's also fun.

I have one master key on my key ring and can access any of my rental units at a moment's notice. I also rekey all the locks to the same key for each unit. This is very convenient for the tenants, saves me the cost of keys and makes organization very easy. Of course, it is not possible to master key locks that use a different key style hence stick to one lock style.

SmartKey

There is a new breed of locks called SmartKey that allows you to rekey without taking the lock apart. These locks have a lot of uses but I do not recommend them for rentals. It is too easy for the tenant to rekey the lock themselves in which case you no longer have access and without the new key, you cannot rekey it again. They are also much more expensive.

Insert functioning key & turn 1/4 turn clockwise.

Insert & remove the SmartKey learn tool. Remove functioning key.

Insert new key & turn 1/2 turn counter-clockwise. Done. Your lock is now re-keyed!

Privacy Locks

Bathrooms use a privacy lock. This means there is a means of locking the door from the inside using the turn button but does not use a normal key. Instead, the outside knob has a small opening that accepts any small item like a paperclip, in case the door is accidentally locked with no-one inside to open it or in case a small child is locked inside.

Note- the screws are visible on the outside of the door as a secondary means of access.

I strongly recommend you do not use these for anything but bathrooms. If used for a bedroom, you will find the door will be smashed in because kids are fooling around or it is locked accidentally.

Passage Door Hardware
Bedroom and closets use passage door hardware. They do not lock at all. They just keep the door latched closed.

Windows

If the windows are old, single glazed, wood or aluminum windows, it is good to upgrade them to modern vinyl units. This is more work than anything we have dealt with previously in this book, will need more tools and so general handyman skills. Having said that, it is not that complicated and something you should strongly consider doing yourself.

If you have not done anything like it in the past, find a friend that has, and will help you with the first one. It is worth paying them to help you. Once you have done one, it will give you the confidence to do the rest yourself, and others in the future.

New windows will help you rent your unit for the best price, will keep the utilities lower and increase the value of your investment.

There are so many variations on existing windows and installation [brick, stucco, siding etc] it is not possible to teach you how to replace a window. Go to YouTube and look for a video with a style similar to yours and follow along.

Heating

If you remember I talked about not providing anything that was not mandatory. Well, heating is mandatory. You must provide heat to all habitable rooms [living room, dining room, family room and bedrooms]. You do not need to provide heat to the kitchen, bathrooms, hallways, laundry etc.

I like to use 'Cadet' wall heaters [available from Home Depot and many other places]. They are inexpensive to purchase and replace, easy to install and inexpensive to operate. If your unit already contains a central heating type system, consider removing it and installing cadet heaters. A central heating system is very expensive to maintain. You might be able to sell the central heating system used and cover the cost to the cadet heaters.

Hardware

You will find you will use the same hardware over and over. It is well worth building up a little stock to the common items to make maintenance easier. Buying in bulk can also save you money. Things like:

- Door locks
- Plumbing parts
- Nails and screws
- Light fixtures

You can also frequent garage sales and flea markets, Habitat Restore, and pick up many of these items at a fraction of the cost.

Sometimes, when I need an item for a unit, I will buy a nice item, install it in my home and install the used item in my rental.

Tools

This is my favorite subject. As I said in my 'About the Author' chapter, I started my career with only hand tools. Over time I have purchased almost every tool in the tool shop. The industry has gotten to the point that if a job can't be done by a power tool, we adjust the job to suit the tools.

The problem we face is if we took all our tools to the job site [rental unit] it would be a large amount of equipment, take up a lot of space and be very vulnerable to theft. Over the years, I have gone full circle and now I have created a toolset that is very versatile and yet very portable. The fact is 90% of the work is done by only 10% of my tools.

Crescent wrench

Channel

lock

Vice Grip

Tool ...Carriers

#1 [Hammer Bag]	#2 [no hammer]	#3 [Electric Tools]
OUTSIDE	OUTSIDE	OUTSIDE
Sissors stout	Glue gen purpose	Lineman pliers
Screwdriver - Phillips slim	Glue wood Full	Snub nose plyers
Screwdriver -Multi	Needle nose plyers	Needle nose pliers Fine & Stout
Wire cutters - yellow/black handle	Screwsdriver small slot/phillips	Electrical tester plug in
Socket driver 7/16 on handle	Screwdriver black phillips hex shaft	Electrical tester no touch x 4
Small pruner cutter	Screwdriver Big slot	Wire slippers x 3
Utility knife - carpet Sharp & Spares	Toothbrush	Utility knife yellow Sharp & Spares
Utility knife - retractable Sharp & Spares	Paint can opener Large & Small	Screwdriver multi
Staple tool long	Pencil-carpenter & #2 Sharp	Screwdrivers small slot x 2
Staple tool short	Countersink bit	
Drywall hole saw	Pincers	INSIDE
Small clamp	Crescent wrench s/m/l [with worm wheel]	Electrical tester 220 wired
Pencil-carpenter & #2 Sharp	Chanel lock medium	Electrical tape black. wire nuts selection
Sheet Metal Cutters yellow	Vice Grip standard [locking grip]	
	Jr Hacksaw	CLEANING SUPPLIES
INSIDE	Drywall Rasp	Windex & paper Towels
Pin hammer	Sissors lightweight	Goo Gone
Claw hammer	File small	Detergent spray - degreaser
Cats claw	Gimlet	Scouring powder - comet
Flat bar		Green scrubber pads
Bit block misc bits Full	INSIDE	Sponges various
Screw / nail box Full	12' torpedo level	Rags & micro fiber
Drill bit set Complete	25' tape	Toilet brush and liquid
Speed sq Yellow	Putty knife s/m/w	Tooth Brush
Tweezers	Chisel 3/8" 1/2" & 1"	Disinfectant - Pine Sol
Razor blade holder	WD 40	Liquid Detergent for mop
Tape measure 16'	Blue masking tape	Razor blades & puttie knife
	Stud finder	Gloves
continued from >>>>>	Head light	Magic errasor
Robo Grip	Lock hole saw	Oven cleaner
Black Electrical Tape	Sanding blocks	Mop & Bucket
Caulking corner	Teflon tape	Broom - stiff
Paint Brush	Black Electrical Tape	Hand brush and Dust pan
	Small socket set	

Materials

Don't fall in love with the property, it is a business and every penny you spend is money out of your profit, out of your pocket. (that was worth repeating!) You do not need top of the line fixtures and fittings. You can find many bargains at yard sales, thrift shops, and resale stores. You can even install items taken from your own home and buy new for yourself.

Look for items like light fixtures, faucets, vanity sinks, door handles and locks, all the little stuff that quickly adds up when you are buying new. Even perfectly good stoves and refrigerators can be had for a song.

I carry the following common items in plastic containers [one for each section]. This covers 95% of the items I need to make repairs.

P a r t s	t o	C a r r y	
Toilet	Plumbing	Electrical	Paint
Wax ring	Water supply flex 2	Light Bulbs 2	Touchup paint cream
Bolts	Shower pole	Light switches 2	Brushes
Flusher valve	Shower head	Outlets 2	Caulk & Gun
Flapper	Drain parts	Plate selection [1 dob sw	Red paint kit [roller, tray & paint]
Toilet Handle	Kitchen faucet	2 out, 2 switch, 2 blank]	White Spray Paint [heater covers etc]
Toilet Roll holder	Lav faucet		
Water supply flex	Sink strainer		Hardware
	Sink & tub plug		Curtain rail and clips
Seat	Water heater drain cap	Light fixture outside	Door locks set
	Water heater element	Cadet heater 220	Smoke detectors 2
	WH element tool & hose	Cadet heater 110	Bug Spray
	Sink Handles		Drain Opening Liquid
			Light Fixture Inside
			Towel Rail & Back Board
			Smoke detectors base

Appliances

Whether you provide appliances or not is up to you, but whatever you provide you will need to maintain. If you provide a refrigerator and it stops working, you will need to pay for a repair person to come and quickly make the repairs or be prepared to buy a new one. You might also be liable for spoilt food. This is definitely not something I know how to repair.

TIP. Write in the Rental Agreement that the specified appliances [write in what appliances are included] are provided as a convenience, AS-IS and the maintenance of such items are the responsibility of the tenant. If they call and say it needs repair, remind them what is written in the Rental Agreement. Ask them if they want you to pick up the appliance so they can get their own.

One option is to provide appliances at an extra cost, say $15 per month each. Then get an inexpensive new unit or a good used unit with a warranty. It should be structured so it pays for itself within a couple of years with the extra charge.

Not providing appliances might put off applicants. Bottom line is to see what your competitor rentals offer and keep in line with what is expected.

Some tenants will have their own fridge and if one is in the unit, you will need to move it out and store it. You could wait until you have an applicant then if they say they want certain items, get them.

Unless it is a high-end rental, they do not need to be new. Craigslist and yard sales have lots very inexpensive.

On move out, often the most unpopular job is cleaning the stove and fridge. It often takes over an hour to clean a stove that appears it was never cleaned since the tenant moved in. The same with the fridge, full of rotting food.....yack. This job is what I call the exception to the rule. Yes, I could do the cleaning but I feel my time is better spent elsewhere – anywhere else.

Move Outs

Photo everything [see flip order] including date and time on the photo.
When someone tells you they are moving out, tell them that is fine but you must give 30 days' written notice [or whatever time period specified in your lease or state]. The time starts when they provide the written notice. This is important because you need to know when the rent stops. If they pay rent beyond this period, you need to refund the prorated amount. If they do not pay for all the notice period, it will come out of their security deposit.

When they turn over the keys and leave the premises, photograph the property making sure the date and time is stamped on every photo **the same day**. Take these photographs BEFORE you remove anything...even rotting food! Do not wait even one day, allowing the tenant to say someone must have broken in and done the damage.

Many landlords get fixated on trash that is left. Yes, you need to document that but what is more important is to take GOOD photos of ALL **damage**. Always assume you will need to present the photos in court to prove damages.

Also, make a list of all damage and missing items. Create a financial accounting of the cost to repair the property back to the same condition as when it was rented – minus normal wear and tear.

Security deposit minus the cost of repairs and rent owing equals the amount of refund or outstanding money owed you. Be fair and be prepared to defend your accounting in court if they sue you in small claims court.

Repairing the Vacant Unit

Now you can start to put the unit back in rentable condition. Every day it is vacant is lost rent/income. Put your sign out front and make sure the front looks tidy.

Work through the unit starting at the front door [first impressions] work back to the kitchen, bathroom, and bedrooms.

Keep the interior tidy at all times. You never know the minute a good prospect tenant will come to the door to see the unit. The tendency is to tear the whole place apart. Materials everywhere. Construction debris accumulates. The place looks a mess. This makes the remodeling process less efficient, even unsafe and most visitors cannot visualize the finished product. Only work on one area at a time, preferably starting at the front door for first impressions.

Store materials at the rear of the unit neatly. Keep tools out of sight in a closet. Add a deadbolt to the closet during the remodel process. Dispose of trash and construction debris as it occurs.

You Find a Tenant

The day arrives that you get someone wanting to rent the unit. Now what? You must have Application Forms ready. Make sure it is a good form and they fill it out completely. One for each adult. Help them if necessary. When completed, look it over and double check it is complete and makes sense.

You need to check their references. We start with a credit check. You will need to find a company that will run a credit report. There is a fee for this and you will charge your applicant this fee which is nonrefundable. Have a receipt book ready. When the report comes back, look it over and make your decision. If you reject the applicant based on the report, you must tell them the reason [in case the report is inaccurate]. If approved, move to the next step which is collecting the first month's rent and security deposit.

Also, call all the previous landlords. They will be unlikely to tell you a lot about a tenant, but will usually answer questions you present them such as;

- How long have they rented from you
- Do they pay rent on time
- How many 3 day notices have your served on them

- Are you evicting them
- Do they have pets
- Have they caused any damage
- Have you had any complaints about them
- Would you rent to them again

If they are to move in mid-month, charge a prorated amount for that month and all of the next month. Collect the money and give a receipt that is very clear what is rent and what is the security deposit.

Create the rental agreement or lease and have them sign it **before they move in**, better still as soon as you approve them, especially if they are not moving in right away. They might change their mind at the last minute and you are back to square one.

Mold

Your state will likely require you give a printed copy of the EPA mold brochure. You can download and print it from the EPA website. The brochure is not printer friendly. It is in color and will use a lot of ink to print. You can get a printer friendly copy from my website www.RentLongview.com

Lead Paint

Properties built before 1978 will also require you give the EPA Lead Paint brochure, again available from the EPA [not printer friendly] or download from my website www.RentLongview.com.

Smoke Detectors

It is important your rental have the required smoke detectors. The requirements vary but usually are one in each bedroom, one in each hall outside the bedroom and one on each level if multi-level.

Smoke detectors come in many price ranges. I always buy new inexpensive units under $6. That way I know I have done everything I can for my tenant's safety and complied with the law.

If you have existing smoke detectors and choose to leave them, install a fresh battery in each one.

Move-In

On move-in day, use a Property Condition form to document the condition of the property. Walk through every room and note any problems then both you and the tenant sign the form. Take photos of every wall and every item in every room. I cannot emphasize this enough. Imagine standing in court after the tenant moves out. The judge asks for photos of all damage and that area before they moved in. You do not know what and where they will damage so you need at least 6 of every room, each wall, the floor, and ceiling. Take close-ups of high-risk items like heaters, stove [inside and out] refrigerator [inside and out].

Keep all the paperwork in a file for this unit. When all move in money is paid and all papers are signed by all adults, hand over the keys, they are now free to move in and you give up the right to enter without their permission.

By the way, the move in money needs to be in a non-stoppable form. Do not accept a personal check or credit card. These can be stopped. Insist on cash, money orders or cashier's check. Let them know in advance this is needed. NO EXCEPTIONS.

Managing the Property

It is in your best interest to maintain the property. This will keep the tenant happy, after all, that is what they are paying rent for. Happy tenants stay longer. Vacancies mean more work, more expenses and less money for you.

Keep a log of everything you do. Note reports of date and time of problems reported by the tenant, and the date, time of what you did to remedy the problem. Remember you are a professional, you are getting paid by the tenant to be professional and if things go wrong, you may need to explain to a judge what happened.

Many landlords spend a lot of time doing credit checks and eviction records. The more you try to get a good tenant, the harder it is to find a tenant to move in and the longer your vacancy and loss of rent.

My policy is to contact the previous landlord and chat with them about the tenant. Go visit the current address. Tell them you forgot to ask them something and poke your nose in the door to see how they currently live. Get inside if you can, ask to use the restroom. The condition of this rental is how your rental will be if they move in.

My main check is CASH. A large security deposit that is. Get a minimum on 1 ½ times the monthly rent. I consider this the eviction money. That is enough to get them out if they do not pay the rent. You must act quickly though if they do not pay. If they have not paid by the 7th, serve a 3 three day notice and evict on the 11th day if not paid in full. If you do not follow this rule they will take advantage of you and drive you nuts. Their problems are not your problems. Trust me on this. NO EXCEPTIONS

Collecting Rents

You could argue that the most important part of the business is collecting rent because this is how we make money and pay our bills. There are many different ways to collect your rent which I will outline.

1. **Collecting rent in person.** This is by far the most effective method. For many years I used this method. I blocked out 5pm to 6pm on the 1st of each month to go around my units and collect the rent. I liked the personal contact with the tenant and get a peek at what is going on inside. If they have any problems, you can see for yourself and make a plan to make the repairs. After we did the rounds, my wife and I would go out for a nice dinner.

The disadvantage is it is time-consuming. Also, it can be annoying if the tenant is not home or says they do not have the rent and you need to return again [and again sometimes].

2. **Have the tenant mail the rent to you**. This is very simple, but tenants tend to send the rent at the last minute or late. It is harder to know if the tenant has a problem paying. Before you know it, it is the 15th and you realize someone has not paid. You call them and they say it is in the mail, but then it is the 20th and still no rent. Now you have problems.

3. **Depositing to your bank account**. You can provide the tenant with deposit slips and they pay directly to the bank. The problem is you need a system with your bank to track who made each deposit and you constantly need to monitor the account until all is accounted for. It is also risky giving out your bank information. It is possible for the tenant to empty your account.

4. **Electronic Payments.** It is possible to have a Credit Card merchant account or PayPal account which the tenant pays into. The main problem with this is there

are fees you have to pay and you still need to monitor it closely.

5. **Direct Debit.** You can set up a special business account with your bank that allows you to withdraw funds from your tenant's bank account each month – [like the utility companies etc do]. There is a modest monthly charge [like $20 no matter how many units you have] but this can be a good system.

6. **12 checks.** I heard of a lady that asked the tenant to give her 12 postdated checks at the start of each year. On the first of each month, she deposits that check.

7. Send out a monthly bill every month to tenants with a self-addressed, stamped [or not stamped], return envelope. They tear off the bottom portion of this bill and mail it back to you in that envelope. Also, on that tear-off portion of the bill, there is a place for them to write in any repairs/concerns they have. I keep these stubs on file. If it ever came about that they complained I didn't fix things to either myself or a judge, I have proof that they have had the opportunity to tell me each month that there was a problem and neglected to do so.

8. Have a locked drop box at a multi-unit building. Give everyone the option of mailing to PO or dropping money order in dropbox. Make one stop at the box and pick up the envelopes.
9. Use ClearNow (directrentdeposit.com) and require tenants to participate with direct rent deposits as part of the lease agreement.
10. Separate bank account [or sub account] for each unit and they deposit it right into the account each month.
11. Some banks will now do "Designated deposit" – tenant tells teller the Landlord's name, teller looks it up, makes deposit, and adds a memo to the deposit with Tenant's house number. This shows on the deposit receipt to Tenant, and shows online for Landlord.
12. Have custom deposit slips with a code for each rental unit on it. Give the deposit slips to the tenants, they deposit the rent in the bank. Check the deposits on-line which also give me date and time stamps. IF LATE they pay a late fee.

Cash vs Check

In today's changing times, technology plays a larger role in the way we do business. More options are available to us in banking, communication and in collecting the rent from tenants.

Just as every property is unique, so is every landlord and his business. How landlords and property managers choose to collect rent varies greatly depending on experience and circumstances. There are a number of payment methods available for you to choose from when it comes to collecting rent from your tenants [see above].

You can accept your rent: In Cash

Accepting rent payments in cash normally means personal contact with the tenant, which can be quite involved at times. You may be thinking, "Cash is the simplest form of payment", but in reality, it can be a royal pain in the neck! Think about the pros and cons and you decide.

The Pros of collecting rent in cash

You don't have to worry about checks bouncing. You don't have to wait for funds to clear your bank account.

The Cons of collecting rent in cash

- Going to the tenant to collect cash. You have to [or have someone else] meet personally with the tenant every month to collect your rent. This can sometimes turn out to be a time-consuming session as it is an opportunity for the tenant to occupy your time with questions, complaints and/or demands concerning the rental property.

- Travel time and expense. What if your rental property is more than a quick hop away?

- Missed appointments. Have you ever heard of a tenant missing an appointment to pay the rent? How about just being late?

- Having the tenant come to you. Some landlords have wised up and don't allow the tenants the ability to waste their time on missed and late appointments and cost gasoline and time driving to rentals to get stuck talking to each tenant about their wish-lists, etc. Instead, the tenant comes to the landlord's home or business with the cash. [They might just want to come in and chat sometimes.] For landlords who prefer their tenants to have 24-hour access to them at home 7-days a week, weekends and holidays, this is a great option!

- Count the money. Remember you should count the cash in front of the tenant to make sure it is all there!
- Security carrying cash is a concern

Don't forget to give the tenant a receipt.

You can accept your rent:
By Check

Collecting rent by check is the method most landlords prefer. It also has its pros and cons, but so does every method.

The Pros of collecting rent by check

- Checks can be mailed.
- Tip: Professional landlords have tenant mail the rent to a PO Box or a management office, not their home.
- It is illegal to pass a bad check.
- It is easier to prove rent was paid late. [By the postmark or even the date the check was written]
- You know where the tenant banks. [This can be useful in the event you have to recover money from the tenant in the future.]

The Cons of collecting rent by check

- Checks bounce when the tenant doesn't have the money in the bank

- Bounced checks incur bank fees that you must then collect from the tenant with a Dishonored Check Notice
- Checks can be stopped by the tenant even after being deposited.

Accepting your rent by Money Order

The Pros of collecting rent by Money Order

- Money orders are not likely to bounce
- Money orders are difficult to cancel
- They are easy to obtain at the Post office, 7/Eleven, Walmart, many drug stores, and any bank.
- They can easily be mailed just like a check, so you do not have to see your tenants in person every month in order to get the rent.

The Cons of collecting rent by Money Order

- Maybe inconvenient for some tenants to go out and buy the money order
- There is a charge for Money Orders

Electronic Rent Collection: Direct Deposit

More and more landlords are making the arrangements with their banks [with their tenants' cooperation] to automatically withdraw a monthly sum from the tenant's bank account to be transferred into the landlord's bank account on a set day every month. This can be an effortless method of rent collection as long as the tenant has the required money in the bank at the time of the transfer. It is an even better situation for the landlord when the tenant is qualified for sufficient overdraft protection.

The Pros of collecting rent by Automatic Withdrawal

- No effort to collect when all is going well.
- Easy to monitor online.
- Not that difficult to set up with most banks

The Cons of collecting by Automatic Withdrawal

- Monthly bank fees to maintain the account
- You have to monitor the account to make sure the rent was transferred

Electronic Rent Collection: Credit and Debit Cards

Many property management companies and even private landlords are accepting the payment of rent by credit and debit cards. Access to this is normally restricted to businesses with merchant accounts to be allowed to accept the major credit cards, but now in today's high-tech environment, just about anyone can have a PayPal account or SquareUp account to enable them to accept credit card payment.

The Pros of collecting rent by Credit and Debit Cards

- Even if it isn't your primary method of collecting the rent, PayPal could enable the tenant to use his credit card[s] to pay you when he otherwise couldn't pay the rent.
- Many management companies have websites that make it easy for tenants to pay their rent online. This is a super convenience for people who are used to paying their bills online.
- Online payments save the time of mailing and can be instantly verified.
- You can use PayPal for billing and Send invoices online, even if you don't have a website. You can also include a payment button in any email you send using Outlook.

The Cons of collecting by Credit and Debit Cards

- By making it easy for the tenant to pay rent by credit card, you could unknowingly have tenants who are headed towards eviction while depending on limited credit to stay afloat.

- Transaction fees. You would be required to pay a transaction fee each time you accept this method of payment. PayPal's transaction fees range from 1.9% to 2.9% + $0.30 USD. This is not a bad deal considering you do not have to pay any other bank fees or other fees associated with having a merchant account.

Fitness and Diet

Yes you read that right, I will talk a little about fitness and diet.

I had a friend who spent several thousand dollars buying the best bicycle he could afford so he could go on long rides and get in shape. The bike was super-efficient and had very little friction etc.

I am no bike rider but was confused why one would spend so much money for the most efficient bike. It seems to me a less efficient bike would give a better work out. That is just my ignorant opinion.

So, having just turned 60, I am not in as good shape as I use to be. Weight has quietly accumulated on my body and getting it off seems impossible. I go on a diet and lose weight, just to put it back on. My downfall is I have a sweet tooth.

Not surprisingly, when I am remodeling a new property or fixing up a unit between tenants, I lose weight from the extra energy and keep my body – well moving. A nice side effect I will gladly accept. A free gym membership.

Difficult Tenants

From time to time, no matter how well I screen my tenants, I end up with a problem tenant – the tenant from hell.

We can, of course evict a tenant by giving them written notice – or can we.

If we have a tenant that has a lease, say a one year lease, you will need to show that they have broken the lease in some way to terminate the tenancy early.

If the tenant is complaining the unit is not habitable [mold, non-working items, insects, pests etc,] it suddenly gets harder to terminate, even if they refuse to pay the rent. We are not permitted to retaliate a tenant's complaints, so we MUST correct ALL items they have complained about, no matter how trivial, wait a while and then use an attorney to help you. Trust me on this one, do not let this happen, by staying on top of maintenance. You will need to do it anyway after you get rid of them.

With bad tenants, it is often worthwhile to pay them to leave – say $1,000 if they leave within 2 weeks [cash for keys]. It is distasteful, but usually cheaper to pay them to leave than to deal with horrid people.

Evicting Tenants

OK, so I left evictions to the end, mostly because it is a last resort. There is nothing worse than an eviction, well actually it is second worse, there is nothing worse than a tenant living in a unit and not paying.

Many landlords have had rentals for years and never needed to evict a tenant. If you have a fair rental at a fair price and treat the tenants well, many will respect you and treat you right. But there is an exception to every rule. Sooner or later you will hit that bad apple.

They often start out as nice people but fall on hard times, or you or your property has a problem and they seize the opportunity to gold dig, suck you for everything they can get away with.

Other tenants are just plain mean. They know the system and play it like a violin. They will say "I know my rights" Sooner or later you will need to evict a tenant.

The first problem is recognizing when it is time. They tell you they have a financial emergency and the rent will be a few days late. They are testing and **training you**. If they get away with it, it will become later and later. They will pay others bills before you. They will buy luxury items out of impulse, knowing you will wait for the rent. DON'T LET THAT HAPPEN. You need a plan and stick to it.

The first defense is to require a large deposit. We call it a security deposit in case they cause damage. I think of it as their eviction deposit. It needs to be enough to cover the cost of evicting your tenant.

You plan needs to be along the lines of:
If rent is not paid by the 7th, you serve a three-day notice to pay rent or quit [no exceptions]. If they do not pay within that three days, you evict them. PERIOD. Only serve a three-day notice if you plan on going through with an eviction. A three-day notice that is not followed up with an eviction is dangerous. They will know they can get away with excuses and your threats are empty. Before you serve the three-day notice, know what you will do if it is not paid. Research the eviction procedure. Have the forms ready to go or have an attorney picked out and ready to act.

Attorney Eviction
The best way to evict a tenant is to use an attorney. Before you ever have a problem, you should have picked out an attorney, know what they charge, how long it takes and what will be needed to win possession of your rental back. Have them check your rental agreement and any legal notices you might use to make sure

they are compatible with your city/county court rules.

Currently, I am paying $400 for my attorney plus the court costs – around $350 and it is taking about three weeks from start to finish. Other areas you will pay more and might take longer.

Make sure the attorney you choose, does a lot of evictions. Actually, the law clerk in the office will likely do all the work, overseen by the attorney and the attorney appears in court.

Doing Your Own Evictions

When I was a landlord in California, I always did my own evictions. I followed a book called "The Eviction Book of California". The court clerks were not easy to work with and they would not give any help. If the application is wrong, they will simply mail it back to me with little clue what is wrong, but if you use the correct forms [which my county clerk had for sale] and follow carefully the rules of the book, it is easy to do yourself.

You still need to pay the court fees and it might take a little longer doing it yourself.

In the county I live now, the court clerk will not provide the forms and that makes it almost impossible to do it myself. Consider sitting in the court when they hear Unlawful Detainer actions. Note if any are done by the landlord and if so catch them on the way out [assuming they seem to know what they were doing] and ask if they will assist you with your first eviction. Even if you never do your own eviction, time spent in the courtroom is very valuable education.

Also, ask at your local landlord association meeting if anyone does their own eviction and would they be your mentor.

An eviction requires several steps. Each step has a waiting period. Know and understand each waiting period and act on the next step the minute you are able.

Are You Paying Attention

This is the second printing of this book. It was originally written two years ago.

Having turned 62 and been in the rental business for over 40 years and made a tidy nest egg, I decided to phase out of the rental management business. Yes against my own advise, I turned over the management of my rental properties to a professional management company, the best in town. My wife and I wanted to do some traveling and this would give us some freedom.

We had a rocky start. The company was not going to run my rentals like I did. The first vacancy I watched what they did. It took 12 days after the move out for the agent to visit the unit. She said she only needs to return the deposit within 14 days so she was on schedule. She returned all the deposit despite there being problems.

- She next scheduled the guys to come and remove the items and trash left.
- Then she scheduled the maintenance supervisor to see what repairs were needed.
- Then the kitchen floor was replaced [out of order] ,

- then a drywall contractor to repair some small holes in the wall.
- Then the painter to paint the unit.
- Then the handyman to install blinds and window screens [I did not want] and towel rails etc,
- then the cleaners to make it ready to advertise
- then she came back and took photos and
- eventually the unit was advertised for rent

This whole process took weeks and they were so picky with the applicants, the total time empty was 12 weeks. This happened each time there was a vacancy.

The monthly disbursement to me soon became not enough to pay the tax and insurance. What a lousy deal.

As soon as we returned from our big trip, I took the property back.

PLAN B

I decided to hire an onsite manager. I was looking for someone that could do all the maintenance or be teachable, and collect the rents.

I found a nice young man that was a little green but very ready to learn. He took the main load off me and every month that goes by, he is able to do more and more with less and less involvement by me. This is in exchange for free rent of a three bedroom apartment. It is a win-win.

Conclusion

There is no better way to earn a good living than by owning rental property. Yes, it is not all roses, but neither is getting up at 6-am, commuting for an hour just to work a job you hate, making someone else a fortune. As a landlord, you will earn your money, but every year you will be building an empire like no other way.

Being self-employed as a rental property owner does not have benefits per say, but your rental empire will surpass any other retirement plan. It is not a 9 to 5 job commitment. You can work your own hours, take long vacations and be master of your own life. I have known several people who have died and not had enough assets to pay for their own funeral. Don't let that be you.

SECTION III

HOUSE FLIPPING

Introduction

This section discusses the process of buying a property for the sole purpose of remodeling it to resell, commonly known as "flipping".

This practice has been made popular by recent DIY programs on TV that tend to glamorize the process, but make no mistake; the process of house flipping is hard work, very stressful and requires a lot of money and skill.

There are a couple of reasons why a person might want to flip a house. The first reason is it is a historic or classical building and a person wants to do the project for the love of the building. The second reason is TO MAKE MONEY. I believe 99% or more fall into the latter and this book deals with this.

Who should flip houses?

Some that start a project have many skills in building and have much time to devote to the project; others take it on in their spare time and have little or no construction skills.

I am not saying to be successful everyone needs to be a builder. It is very desirable if you have knowledge, skill and time to do much of the work, but it is not mandatory. You can be very successful by taking on the role of project manager and contract out the work to professionals. An advantage of this is you can run the project part-time, possible holding a full-time job to keep the money coming in during the project. Or you can manage several projects at the same time. The main disadvantage of contracting most or all of the work is it will cost more money so you will make less and increase your risk of losing money.

Money/Finances

I must up front take the time to talk about money as this is the single most important subject. They say it takes money to make money. I am not sure who said it but they must have been house flippers.

You need money to purchase the house, you need money to pay for the upgrades and you need money to carry the property while you own it, items like insurance, utilities, and loan.

Many flippers are forced to borrow some or all of the funds. This is understandable because it takes vast amounts of money to complete a project and if you already had vast amounts of money you wouldn't need to flip houses. However, the more you borrow, the harder it is to make a profit assuming you have to pay interest on your loan and if you do not need to pay interest please tell me where it is coming from so I can get some.

In order to flip houses you do not need to be a math major or an accountant, but you do need to be able to budget, project costs and analyze financial progress constantly to avoid financial disaster. You also need a basic understanding of all likely costs.

The expenses fall into the follow classes:
Purchase

Fix up
Carrying costs
Selling expenses

Purchase includes such additional items as home inspection, termite inspection, up-front loan fees and points, appraisal and escrow fees.

Fix up costs must include all labor, materials, permits, dump costs including money kept aside for unforeseen surprises.

Carrying costs will include mortgage or loan payments, insurance, utilities.

Selling expenses will include Realtor fees [often 6% of sales price] staging costs [often 1 – ½% of sales price] escrow fees, transfer taxes, property gains tax.

The selling expenses are the most often forgotten item that can turn a profit into a loss. It is possible to sell without a realtor and save some money but this is not usually a good move. A Realtor will often generate more offers, faster that are higher [more on this later].

Do you have the right stuff?

As we have said, you do not need to be a builder to do house flipping but assuming you are not a builder; you must have a general understanding of buildings and the construction process in order to communicate and negotiate with contractors.

You must have enough time to manage the project. The more time you spend at the property, the more efficient the project will go, the faster it will go and the cheaper it will be.

You need to understand contractors. As we have said, they are not likely waiting for you to call so they can come right over. There is a pecking order. A contractor will take care of big customers first. At the start, you are a small fish wanting a small job done for the least amount of money. Not surprisingly, you will not be top of their list. As you get into the business, if you frequently use the same contractors, have a professional rapport with them and pay on time, you can become their big fish that gets preferential treatment. But that takes time. You need the contractor to be your partner, not your enemy. Be nice to them.

If you are lucky enough to have construction skills, and you have the time to devote to the project, then you can save a lot of money on labor charges. Almost 50% of a job is labor and profit so you stand to save this, assuming you can create an end product of the same quality. The other factor of course is time. Doing the work yourself will take more time, lots more time. If it takes an additional 3 months by doing the work yourself, you will need to budget three months of loan payments so calculate this carefully. Consider doing some work yourself and getting sub-contractors to speed some slow jobs along.

If you hire one contractor to do 100% of the work from A to Z, that contractor is referred to as a General Contractor and you are their clients. If you hire out each trade, you become the General Contractor and they Sub-Contractors. If you hire out various projects to several General Contractors ie one for an addition and one for the bathroom remodel and kitchen and each hires Sub Contractors, you become the Project Manager.

Whatever hat you wear, you need to be as professional as the contractors you hire. Give them respect, be prepared with dimensions, specifications, plans and handle problems as a normal part of work, not as a major crisis. Contractors will treat you like you deserve and will even walk off the job if you are not pleasant.

Selecting the right house

Assuming you are not a contractor [and even if you are] the first project should be not too challenging [cosmetic fixer] with the goal of breaking even. Any profit should be considered a bonus. Aiming for a big profit on your first project is not a good idea. Many flippers end a project exhausted and disappointed at the net profit because they were not mentally prepared for the amount of work and stress and were hoping for big money that did not materialize. Consider any profit you make on the first project to be a bonus.

There are many factors that will determine your net profit and most are out of your control. Having a property that looks good at the end is within your control, but the state of the market is not. Factors that will affect price include time of year, numbers of houses for sale in the neighborhood, state of the economy, job availability, interest rates.

You could have the best house in the area but if there are no jobs or the interest rates are high, selling can be very difficult.

It is important to not only look at houses but to look at neighborhoods. You need to get a feel whether the area is improving or declining. How do we do this? You need to look at the area for the following:

Number of houses for sale, is the market saturated: a buyer's market.

Condition of houses, are they run down or are lots of people fixing them up.

The availability of jobs in the area, are businesses closing and jobs hard to find or are new businesses opening up with good opportunities.

How is crime? Are their drug dealers on the corner or do the homes show pride of ownership?

Select a house that has room to grow. You must find out what the price range is for the area. In the past two years find out what the top price has been for sales and what the bottom price is. Do not expect to exceed or meet top price. You must make the most of your profit when you buy ie buy an undesirable home for a very low price and plan on turning around the negative features into positive selling points during your remodel. Pay little attention to the listing or asking price, this means nothing. You need to know what properties actually SOLD for. This is public record which a good realtor will be able to find out.

Do not overbuild for the area. If all the properties are in a small price range [ie between

$300,000 and $375,000] it would be difficult to sell your house for more than $375,000. If you can find a home in a mixed neighborhood, [ie where homes range from $300,000 to over a million dollars] then you have a good chance of making a profit. I recently drove a new neighborhood. It had many big homes, well-manicured and in the upper price range. There were other homes that were small, overgrown and no pride of ownership and a much lower price range. This area is prime for flipping because there is room to increase the price.

Before you can determine what to buy, you must have a fairly accurate idea of what remodel costs are. You need to know how much a new roof costs, a kitchen remodel, a bathroom remodel, drywall costs, painting costs, floor covering, etc, etc and it must be realistic. THIS IS THE MOST CRITICAL AREA. Do not wing it. Do not go by the seat of your pants. Knowledge is critical. You can purchase books on estimating. You can Google "contractors estimating handbook".

Project worksheet

It is a good idea to create a basic project worksheet. Fill out the worksheet for each property you visit that you think may have merit. This will help you decide if it has potential. Keep all worksheets as you will refer back to them to save making the same calculations over and over again. A simple worksheet may look like the example below but feel free to create and develop your own. If you do it on a spreadsheet, it can calculate the costs for you automatically.

Address 123 Main Street		City Old York		
HOA no	Sq Ft 1800	Beds 3	Baths 2	Age 1980
Property asking price $ 299,000		Offer price $ 235,000		Accepted price $ 250,000
Comp High $ 425,000		Comp Low $ 235,000		Comp Average $ 390,000
Work	**Size /#**	**Unit Cost**	**Total Cost**	
Roofing sq ft	Na			
Exterior	Na			
Windows & Doors	8	250	2,000	
Demo	1	500	500	
Kitchen	1	15,000	15,000	
Bathrooms	2	5,000	10,000	
Plumbing	1	1,000	1,000	
Electrical	1	1,500	1,500	
HVAC	1	4,000	4,000	
Drywall wall & ceiling	2,000	1.5	3,000	
Paint & décor	6,000	.75	4,000	

Tile sq ft	300	4	1,200		
Floor coverings sq ft	1,800	4	7,200		
Permits	450	450	450		
Landscaping	1	1,000	1,000		
Addition sq ft	0	120	0		
Total cost of work			50,850		
Purchase price			250,000		
Purchase expenses			1,000		
Loan Payments [estimated 6 months]			9,000		
Realtor fees [6% of sales price]			24,000		
Closing cost			1,000		
15% emergency			7,500		
Total cost of project			334,350		
Staging [1%]			4,000		
Projected selling price			400,000		
Projected net Profit			52,650		

The two big obstacles

You have selected what you think is the right house at the right time in the right neighborhood. But can you overcome the two big obstacles? The mortgage and the realtor selling costs.

How long has this property been on the market? Perhaps several months. When you commit to buying the house, you are locked into paying the mortgage until you sell it again and close the escrow. Escrow alone are typically two months plus, so from day one you are locked into 2 months mortgage and all the time to find the buyer which is a complete unknown. Ask your realtor what the average "days on the market" is i.e. how long a typical house takes to sell. This is only a guide but it is the best we have. Add that time to your mortgage commitment and see how much you are committed to.

If your mortgage payment is $1,500 per month, days on the market is 120, you are committed to $6,000 which has to come right off the top of your profit.

Realtor fees are typically 6% of the selling price. If you expect to sell for $400,000 the realtor fee will be $24,000 not to mention Escrow fees and closing costs. Add this to our mortgage commitment and we are locked into about $30,000 coming right off the top of any sales price.

Project Timing

Assuming you take out a mortgage or loan to purchase the property, you will likely have a monthly payment to add to your expenses. The longer the project, the less you will profit. Every month that goes by, will cost you.

Having said that, planning on finishing the work fast and selling quickly is foolhardy. Planning on doing all the work fast will increase costs and frustrations and may not end up faster in the long run. All work must be done in the correct order with lots of planning. It would be ideal if the painter comes in as soon as the drywall is complete, but in actual practice, contractors are not likely to be sitting around waiting for you to call. Good contractors are very busy and you will have to wait your turn. Lousy contractors may be able to come right away but you will regret employing bad contractors. Family and friends may be willing to help but will they do good work and do you want to risk falling out with family and friends.

It is important to research the area to see when houses are easier to sell and get the best price. This is often in the summer when people are more likely to go house hunting, kids are out of school and changing to new schools is easier. To plan on selling fast will likely mean settling on a lower price, which translates to lower profit.

There can be some tax benefits to holding on to the property for two years. Consider renting out the property for 21 months. Talk to your tax advisor about this.

Purchase Examples

Let's look at some examples of houses on the market to see which is a good gamble.

House 1 is in an older neighborhood with lots of development indicating the market is improving. It needs a new kitchen and master bathroom and tiles in the guest bathroom. It needs new carpet throughout, a new front door and lots of landscaping.

House 2 is in an older part of town with a lot of houses on the market and no jobs in the area. Houses are cheap but selling will be a problem. It needs less work but the margins are very thin.

House 3 is in a good area and this is the cheapest in the neighborhood. A tenant has just been evicted and the place is a mess with garbage all over and graffiti on the walls. The kitchen is nice and just needs a new countertop. The bathrooms all need gutting and starting over and it needs a new roof.

House 4 is in a good area but is very small. It needs a master bedroom & bathroom addition to compete with other houses nearby.

House 5 is a great house in a good area and the price range is very wide giving a good opportunity to increase its value. The kitchen and bathrooms all need gutting and all the rooms need stripping the drywall and starting from scratch. Lots of tile and carpets with finishes.

House 6 is a nice house with nasty curb appeal. Mostly it needs rebuilding the front porch and new landscaping. New carpets and paint inside.

House 7 is a one bedroom house in a good area. It needs complete internal remodel with 2 new bedrooms and one bathroom.

	House 1	House 2	House 3	House 4	House 5	House 6	House 7
Asking $	100,000	55,000	265,000	675,000	1,213,000	219,000	450,000
Potential $	200,000	95,000	365,000	815,000	1,485,000	299,000	875,000
Fixup $	25,000	18,000	47,000	84,000	67,000	12,000	150,000
Realtor & Staging	14,000	6,650	25,550	57,050	103,950	20,930	61,250
Mortgage	3,500	1,925	9,275	23,625	42,455	7,665	15,750
Misc.	2,000	1,100	5,300	13,500	24,260	4,380	9,000
Net Profit	**55,500**	**12,325**	**12,875**	**(38,175)**	**34,335**	**35,025**	**189,000**
Down payment	10,000	5,500	26,500	67,500	121,300	21,900	45,000
Total outlay	40,500	26,525	88,075	188,625	255,015	45,945	219,750
Return on Outlay	137%	46%	15%	-20%	13%	76%	86%

Study these different scenarios and decide which one you would buy.

When you have found a potential property

Research comps [properties sold] of similar houses in the area to get a realistic idea of the potential selling price. Visit the city or county Building Department to make sure there are no code violations on file or outstanding enforcement action. Talk to the Planning Department to make sure there are no zoning or neighborhood problems. Photograph every room from every angle to allow remodel planning during escrow. Measure every room, length and width including bathrooms and hallways. Create remodel ideas, a rough budget, and realistic timeline.

Make a low ball offer with a long contingency period. Contingencies include home inspection, contractors review, city/county research, financing. A contingency says you make your offer "subject to" the approval of inspection reports within say 30 days. This means that even if your offer is accepted and you open escrow, you can exercise your contingency and terminate the deal without any penalty.

With a contingent offer, you can safely make low ball offers on all kinds of properties. Once one is accepted, you do your thorough research and within the contingency period make your final decision whether to buy or not. I have used this method a lot. Once you have an accepted offer, you control the deal. If things do not look good, you can reduce your offer if necessary or terminate.

Financing

When you make your offer, assuming you do not have all cash, make it a part of the offer that the seller carries all or part of your purchase price with say 10% down. You only need a 12-month loan and could be interest only at the going bank rate. This can make the purchase much faster because there is no bank approval needed, you can skip the appraisal which could be several hundred dollars and no points which could be say 2% of the loan or $2,000. As you can see, all this can save you thousands of dollars.

Home Inspection

As soon as your offer is accepted, arrange for a Home Inspection. Make sure you attend the inspection. Ask how long the inspection will take and plan on spending the first half of the time with your own agenda which is to photo everything and measure everything.

By photographing everything I mean every wall, the ceiling, floor, door, window, light fixture and any other significant item in the room. It should be about a dozen photos for every room. Also, the exterior making sure every inch of the exterior is covered. Lastly the attic and subfloor as best you can.

By measure, I mean the lot size, the external building size, the setbacks, each room size, each window size. Pay special attention to the kitchen dimensions in case new cabinets are needed. Make note of the location of the external faucets and electric outlets.

Test every window to make sure they open and close smoothly and do not leak air. Check the latch works. Open and close every door. Look to see if the gap around the door is even. An uneven gap means the house has or is moving [settling].

When this is done, tag along with the inspector and ask as many questions that you can think of so you get a feel of what the inspector's personal opinion is.

During Escrow

Once the contingency period has ended and you are committed to the purchase, your work begins. Do not wait until escrow close to start planning. You cannot of course, go in the property and start physically making changes, but there is plenty you can do.

Study the photos and measurements you took earlier and create a list of work you feel is needed. Create floor plan to scale. Use graph paper if you are not use to creating plans. You will be surprised that you are able to create a plan. One plan as it is when you buy it and a second plan what you intend to do [before and after]. If you feel this is not necessary, think again. Every hour you spend in preparation and planning can save several hours during the remodel. If you are unable to draw the plans, spend the money and have a professional blueprint service create them for you.

Create a list of all work for each room, outside and yards. The list must be comprehensive and complete down to how many sq. ft. of drywall, paint, flooring, tiles etc. and the quality of materials. Get several bids from contractors and or Sub Contractors for each trade.

Create a budget based on the bids. List everything in the budget and include at least 15% for unforeseen problems. This 15% is not a number you use to compensate for sloppy estimating or just overspending, it is only for unforeseen emergencies, items that may appear when you open the walls and major items come to light that could not have been anticipated.

Visit the Building Department again to see what kind of permits they require based on the work you have planned. Do not shy away from taking out permits. The building inspector can be very helpful in advising about correct work methods and when you come to sell, it is a big selling point to be able to show that all the work is permitted and signed off by the local jurisdiction. If you do not take out necessary permits, you risk getting caught and having lengthy delays and hefty penalties. If you are hiring contractors, the building inspector is your best friend to ensure the work is done correctly. Do not make final payment to contractors until the Building Inspector has passed that work.

Some permits can be obtained instantly "over the counter" at the building department by filling out the form and paying the fee, but other work may need to go through 'plan check', which needs several copies of your plan and specifications and several weeks delay. That is why you need to do this research early so it does not delay the start of work after you close escrow.

If your property is in an area that is controlled by a Home Owners Association, often referred to as an HOA, review the CC&R's [Covenants, Conditions and Restrictions] and any rules that apply. Often they control any changes you make to the outside including paint colors. Be sure you understand the rules and do not break any of them.

You will want to start work the day escrow closes because every day you own the property, it is costing you money. For this reason, you should set up delivery of the dumpster & schedule the demo crew. It is important you have the dumpster on site when you demo, otherwise, you will need to double handle the debris and it will look bad from the street and for the neighbors/HOA. Make sure the utilities will be on starting the day escrow closes.

Time Line

This is where the magic occurs. This is where the professional/successful flipper is separated from the amateurs. Create a "timeline" based on the list below in that order. DO NOT CHANGE THE ORDER unless you have a very good reason. Each job has consequences on the other jobs. Timelines for work inside and outside can be separate but there are some areas that overlap.

1 Start Building Permits & HOA Approvals
2 Dumpster delivery
3 Demo & remove debris
4 Structural changes [opening up kitchen etc]
5 Order kitchen cabinets, Carpeting, Hardwood
      Flooring, tiles etc
6 Hardscaping [pathways and driveway]
7 Start greening up grass & plant large shrubs to get established
8 Additions [if any]
9 Plumbing
10 Roofing
11 Electrical & HVAC
12 Windows
13 Drywall
14 Install Bath Tub/showers
15 Finish carpentry including baseboard, trim, doors & crown molding
16 Siding / Stucco
17 Paint inside & outside
18 Tile, vinyl, carpet and Hardwood flooring

19 Landscaping
20 Install Kitchen cabinets, vanities & toilets
21 Finishes [mirrors, outlet plates, towel rails, light fixtures, hardware etc]
22 Staging

Time Line Explained

1. **Start Building Permits & Home Association Approvals**. Failure to start this early will result in delay and frustration. A successful project is all about preparation, preparation, and more preparation.

2. **Dumpster delivery**. You do not want to double handle any debris so arrange for its delivery the day you close escrow. Everything should go directly into the dumpster to keep the job site clean, safe and professional.

3. **Demo & remove debris**. Do the entire demo at one time. Have all the needed tools including hammers, sledgehammer, crowbar, saws-all [reciprocating saw], wheelbarrow, floor tile blade. Be sure to arrange the utility power to be on and in your name for the first day of ownership. The only exception to the demo up front is windows and doors. Do not remove windows and external doors until the new windows are delivered for security reason.

4. **Structural changes** [opening up kitchen etc]. Knock out any walls that are to be opened up but make sure they are not "load bearing" if you are not sure, get professional help from a contractor in deciding if a wall is load bearing. Even if a wall is load bearing, it can still be opened up if beams etc are correctly designed to transfer the loads. Take professional advice on this.

5. **Order kitchen cabinets, Carpeting, Hardwood Flooring, windows, tiles etc**. Once the demo is complete, mark out the floor and walls to indicate where new materials will start and end. Once marked, measure accurately and calculate the amount of materials needed. Allow for mistakes and waste. The amount to add will depend on your skill level and the material being used. Talk to your supplier for advice on this.

Kitchen cabinets and windows can often take several weeks to be ready so it is critical these are ordered early. Ask if they will delay delivery until you are ready so it is not in the way and risk damage, theft and save clutter on the job site. It is critical enough tiles, flooring etc be ordered all at one time. Ordering more of an item later may risk not an identical match.

6. **Hardscaping** [pathways and driveway]. Getting the drive, paths, and patios done early

will help the job go easier, especially in bad weather.

7. **Start greening up grass & plant large shrubs** to get them established. The bigger the plants, the more expensive they are. Getting them in early and allowing them to get established is a good idea. Be sure to put up barriers so delivery trucks and workers do not damage them. If the grass is not too bad, but just needs greening up, add additional seed and keep watering. Get this started early, from day-one if possible. You will be surprised how good grass can look if mowed neatly, edged, watered and fed [fertilizer]. If it turns out to be lousy grass, you can still go to plan B and use sod, rock or whatever plan B is near completion.

8. **Additions** [if any] are slow and expensive so think very carefully before getting into this. Not for the first time flipper. Permits are always needed for additions and consider hiring one reputable contractor to do the complete addition from start to finish.

9. **Plumbing** needs to be done before any roofing if vents are to go through the roof. Plan on doing all the plumbing work at one time from start to finish.

10. **Roofing** must be done before any electrical work, insulation, and drywall, however, if the

roof is actually leaking and causing damage, it must be moved up to number one.

11. **Electrical & HVAC**. These are trades that need specialists and should be completed before insulation and drywall.

12. **Windows** make a big difference to a project. If your project has single glazed windows, this is a high priority for comfort, economy, and convenience. Allow plenty of time for them to be made and delivered. Do not assume they are standard size and will be in stock.

13. **Drywall**. Once all the above is complete and it is critical it is 100% complete, you can drywall where necessary including tape and texture.

14. **Install Bath Tub/showers**. Depending on what you are doing, bathtubs may need to be installed before or after the drywall. Check on this early.

15. **Finish carpentry** including baseboard, trim, doors & crown molding can be installed once the drywall is complete. Do not let this get left to the end.

16. **Siding/stucco** work can be done at any time up to this point but must be after windows and external doors are installed and before final landscaping.

17. **Paint inside & outside**. Have the colors picked out well in advance with the required quantities based on square footage to be covered. Remember a second coat is often needed and prime bare wood. Painting before flooring, cabinets, fixtures and fittings are installed makes painting easier and looks cleaner.

18. **Tile, vinyl, carpet and Hardwood flooring** must be left late so they do not get damaged by other trades. By now the project is almost over.

19. **Landscaping**. Finish any landscaping that could not be done earlier [near windows, siding, stucco or painted areas].

20. **Install Kitchen cabinets, vanities & toilets**. This is an exciting time as it all seems to come together at this point. Putting the cabinets in after the floor is faster and makes a cleaner look.

21. **Finishes** [mirrors, outlet plates, towel rails, light fixtures, hardware etc]. The finishes take a surprising amount of time but can be the most rewarding. Plan on cleaning everything until everything shines. Windows and mirrors must be spotless, carpets vacuumed, kitchen and bathrooms sparkling. Use a cleaning service if you are too exhausted to give this 100%.

22. **Staging** can make a big difference and sells a house faster and for more money. Staging defines the suggested uses of rooms or areas of a room, highlights the best features of the house and minimized its faults. Talk to several staging companies and select one that has the right items for your type of home. Staging companies often charge a percentage [often 1% or more] of the sales price so there are no upfront fees.

Alternatives to Realtors

You can consider trying to sell the property yourself and save up to 6%. This is called FSBO [For Sale By Owner]. This is to be considered very carefully. How do potential buyers write up the contract? Buyers are nervous about this and could hinder a potential deal. It will not be in MLS [Multiple Listing Service] that realtors use to find properties for sale.

Companies like 'Help U Sell' or 'Assist 2 Sell' charge much less than Realtors because you show the property but they do the marketing and help the potential buyers write the contract. You do need the MLS package to get the realtor exposure.

Escrow Closes

This is it. Congratulations. Block out your time until the project is complete. Plan on working every day if you are doing some of the work and visiting the property every day to monitor progress and quality if others are doing the work. No vacations, no days off. Every day you own the property you are paying the mortgage [if you needed a mortgage to do the project].

Curb Appeal

When finished, the home must be appealing enough to get prospective buyers to get out of the car and view the property. Even those who take a closer look, if the curb appeal is bad, they will view the property with a negative attitude or be thinking 'low ball offer'.

Curb appeal comes down to good landscaping, nice paint job and an attractive house profile. Ugly house features need to be upgraded to make it into an attractive feature. More difficult unattractive features may be able to be disguised by a well-placed tree or bush but this is not the best solution.

More often than not, removal or trimming large trees and bushes is needed to get the correct visual balance and allow the home to be seen from the road. Add a picket or decorative fence.

A new attractive front door is an easy way to upgrade the front and make it more welcoming. Shutters, window boxes, light fixtures and even water features can all be added to get the desired effect. For the low end remodel, a strong red or similar paint job can draw attention away from a plain exterior.

What to Upgrade

They say that kitchens and bathrooms sell houses. These are also the most expensive area's to remodel. Upgrades are based more on functional obsolescence than being broken or worn out. This is a fancy way of saying it is outdated or out of fashion.

Kitchens

The modern trend is marble counter tops, travertine flooring, stainless steel appliances and recessed lighting. The cabinets need to reflect the modern look and feel. The extent of the remodel will depend on the price range. The upper price housing should have all new cabinet's, upper and lower. Affordable housing can have remarkable transformation by replacing the cabinet doors, drawer fronts and counter at a fraction of the cost, mess and time.

Open plan is in. Consider opening up the wall from the kitchen to the living space and installing a breakfast bar. This is good for entertaining, makes the cook feel less isolated and makes the living space feel larger and more "homey". This may require relocating the appliances but it is often the biggest transformation you see when you first enter the front door.

The layout of the kitchen is important. Don't necessarily settle for the same layout as existing. There are a lot of books on kitchen layout but the basic rule is to have a small work triangle between the sink, stove, and fridge. If you are a good cook, stand in the space and imagine you are cooking a big meal. Make sketches as you imagine preparing and cleaning up from your meal. If you are not an avid cook, ask someone to help you. You will spend a lot of money on the kitchen and it would be a crime to end up with a poor layout.

Gas cooking is preferred to electric. Make the change if necessary. Be sure to design a dishwasher and garbage disposal. Be sure internal corners allow enough room for the cupboard doors and drawers to open in both directions. Do not install carpet in the kitchen. Travertine floor tiles are popular and easy to clean.

Granit counters are in fashion and likely to stay popular for a long time. Slab granite is more desirable than granite tile. Finish off the kitchen with stainless steel appliances to make it move in ready and irresistible to the ladies or the cook of the family. This is a chance to get your buyers emotional about your home.

Bathrooms

The master bathroom needs to more than just a functional room. Large tile showers, double sink vanity, careful choice of lighting. Be sure you keep your theme the same, i.e. fixtures all brass or all chrome. A whirlpool tub can win over many home buyers and this should be a high priority if feasible. Small master suites may need to be extended to give the correct feel. Small pokey master bathrooms are OUT. The ultimate shower will have room for two people and have jets that come from more than just above.

It can be very hard to decide if a bathroom should have just a facelift or a complete gut and restart. Often it will be in good condition but just dated. The very first opinion when you and others first see it will often be the best decider. If in doubt, rip it out. Don't get cheap in bathrooms. It is easy to go the easy route and ruin a flip by leaving an older bathroom. The hall bathroom does not need to be as elaborate but needs to contain a bathtub and shower to appeal to families. A decent size vanity will allow plenty of room for toiletries, towels etc.

A guest powder room near the front door only needs a sink and toilet and elaborate mirror and lighting. Consider an elegant pedestal or vessel sink   here.

Walls & Ceilings

It almost goes without saying that all the walls and ceiling must be flat and smooth. Texture is the modern finish. If the plaster has cracks, spend some time in filling the cracks so they are no longer visible even with close examination. If there are a lot of cracks or poor plaster may require flattening the complete surface with drywall mud. Apply a thin coat with a very wide drywall knife, allow to dry and sand smooth.

Inspect carefully and re-apply to any imperfections. It may need three, four or even five coats to get it perfect but it is well worth the time and it is very inexpensive. The alternative is to remove the drywall and re-plaster. This is more expensive but gives a better finish. It also allows you to inspect and correct damaged framing, upgrade the wiring and insulation if necessary. Get bids to re-drywall prior to knocking off the old wall surface. The cost may be more than you expected and extend the length of the job considerably.

Inspect the baseboard and door molding. If they are damaged, replace them. If they are not consistent, replace it all. If you are replacing trim, paint the walls and paint the trim before installing them. It will give a very crisp clean look. Caulk and touch up the gaps to finish off.

Consider adding crown molding to entertaining rooms and even the master bedroom. Wood trim and paint are amongst the easiest and cheapest ways to upgrade a property.

Color Schemes

Walls must be painted with a neutral color in pastel shades. Do not pick strong aggressive colors, even as an accent wall. The trim must be a different but complementary color to look good. Paint a small area of wall and trim and let dry. View in all lights and make changes if it is not good.

For the actual painting, spraying is faster and easier [and cheaper], but hand brushing [which is time-consuming and therefore more expensive] provides a thicker coat which provides better protection by penetrating deeper into the wood and crevasses.

Most people feel the painting is easy, that anyone can do it. Painting is pretty easy but most people fall short of a good paint job. There is a definite technique to painting, starting with the right equipment [ask at your paint supplier for advice]. Paint in the direction of the [wood] grain and end with several long strokes, looking for drips, runs and dribbles around corners. When done, stand back and correct any imperfections visible from different angles. Be sure the light is very good or you will miss problems.

Flooring

Choose the new flooring for your project early. Look under carpets to see if there is hardwood. Hardwood flooring is very popular and exposing existing hardwood can be a good way to go even if it needs to be re-finished.

These days, hardwood floors in the entertaining rooms. Laminate flooring is ok for economy housing but upper-end housing needs high-quality flooring. Use travertine in the kitchen, bathrooms, and laundry and new carpet in the bedrooms.

Finishing Touches

Light fixtures and door hardware are simple and inexpensive upgrades and allow you to keep the theme the same throughout the home. Be sure all tools and leftover materials are completely removed. Keep the landscaping very tidy and grass mowed and green. Fresh flowers and a pleasing sent make a house homely and appealing. Be sure the address is posted on the front and clearly visible from the street so you can be found. Add smoke detectors in each bedroom and in each hallway.

The home must be 100% ready so the people feel they would move in that day.

Choosing Contractors

The irony of choosing contractors is the good ones are booked up but the bad one's can come right away. There is never better advice than to talk to friends for contractors they have used and liked. They must hold a state contractor's license for the type of work they will be performing. The trick is getting several to come and give you a bid. The more organized you are, the easier it is for them to give an accurate price. If you give them too many variables, they will not be able to give an accurate bid and without locking in on prices you will be writing [so to speak] a blank check. You might accept the best price, only to find they are using shoddy materials, or it does not include materials at all.

One of the biggest challenges is getting a contractor to show up when you need and when they promise. You have to consider the contractor's schedule and discuss this when they give their bid. Get everything in writing including their contractor's license number, city license if needed, a full specification of work and materials and timing.

Never, Never, Never give final payment until all work is 100% complete and signed off by the city/county inspector and or Home Owners Association.

Common Mistakes

Not having a dumpster on site when doing demo making double work and clogging up the site.

Ordering materials or cabinets late in the project and having to wait for delivery holding up all work.

Performing work out of order – painting after flooring is installed at best extra work is involved protecting the floor and at worst the risk of damaging the floor.

Not specifying work in writing to be performed by the contractor so you do not get what you want for the cost you expected.

Making changes to work once work has started. Change orders gobble up money.

Not using reputable contractors, often slowing the job and sometimes having to re-do work.

Paying contractors final payment before they have finished all the final details.

Being underfunded. You must have enough money to cover labor, materials, mortgage and utilities for 6 months and 15% for unforeseen problems.

Not having a clear plan of all work with detail descriptions.

Doing Work Yourself

If you have skills, feel free and plan on doing some or all of the work yourself. It must be of high quality and in a reasonable amount of time if you have loan payments. You can consider employing helpers and perhaps some skilled help and act as general contractor. You will need to get workers comp insurance and withhold taxes etc. Be very careful about paying hourly labor under the table or as independent contractors. This can come back to bite you.

No one will take care of the work like you will. No one will shop for good deals on materials like you will. No one will show up and put in 100% every day like you will.

DIY Saving

Assuming you are not a contractor or even a good handyman, there are still things you cans and probably should do yourself.

Demolition and debris removal. Chances are you will be more careful at demo than a contractor. Sloppy demolition can cause damage to nearby areas not needing work. If you are changing the cupboards in the kitchen, consider removing them carefully in one piece and donating them to Habitat to Humanity or other charity or install them in the garage or workshop to appeal to hobby buyers.

Painting is not rocket science and can make a good family project.

Daily cleanup. You can negotiate a better price from your contractor by offering to do the daily cleanup. A clean job site is easier to work in and this can translate to a cheaper and faster job. Be sure the job site is secure. If workers leave the tools and equipment overnight, it saves time each day and ensures they will come back tomorrow.

Runs to the store. A lot of billing hours can be saved by you running to the store and keeps the job running faster. Provide coffee or other drinks to save trips to the donut shop.

Final cleaning needs to be completed prior to showing the property and a good cleaning job can make a job sparkle.

Landscaping. If minimal is needed to the yards, you can do the mowing and watering. Nurseries can give all the information and advice you need about plants. Make a sketch with dimensions and talk to them. They will be happy to create a balanced and full yard. If the grass turns out to be undesirable, sod is a fast way to make a green lush lawn.

Fences can define space and these days they can be purchased ready makeup in 8' sections. Just dig a hole, add a post, cement and just add water. Use a line to keep it straight. Picket fences add to curb appeal and can lead to a looker falling in love with their dream home. Anytime you can make the looker emotionally involved in a property, their logic can go out of the window and you have them hooked.

When the Work is Finished

Now the work is finished, it is time to put the property on the market. You need to visit all the properties for sale in the area to see what you are competing with. You need to research with your Realtor all the completed sales in the area to get a realistic idea of what houses are selling for.

Do not price your property above all the rest. Pitch it just below the top so you are sure to get lots of lookers. You can consider offering to carry a small amount of financing, an amount equal to the profit you stand to make. This is a forced savings plan and will make it easier to sell to the buyers needing a smaller down payment. If the appliances are not new, offer a homeowners warranty [insurance] for one year. It is fairly inexpensive and it gives the buyers peace of mind.

Success or Failure

Do not count your chickens until escrow closes. A deal is not a deal until you get your money. Assuming you have made a profit, what is a success? $20,000 for three months work is a success. It is nice to make lots of money and that will come but you must learn to walk before you start to run.

Sample Specification
Living room

Demo
Remove all carpeting, padding and tack strip including padding staples. All debris to be removed from the site.

Strip all wallpaper from walls and ceiling down to bare drywall, and haul away debris.

Remove all window treatments and haul away. Remove baseboard and door trim and haul away.

Drywall
Repair any damaged drywall [approx. 20 sq. ft.] and coat smooth all wall and ceiling imperfections.

Apply knockdown texture finish to a style approved by the customer [650 sq. ft.].
Remove all debris ready for painting.

Painting
Contractor to inspect all surfaces to be painted, provide any necessary minor filling of holes, cracks and defects with flexible caulking.

Paint all walls, ceiling and trim with Duncan Edwards paint [650 sq. ft.]. Walls to be flat, woodwork and trim to be semi-gloss. Adequate coats to be applied to cover the surface to the client's satisfaction for the price quoted.

The flooring, windows and door to be protected from overspray or roller splatter and these surfaces to be left as clean when completed as when the painter starts work. All masking tape to be removed.

All debris to be removed from the job. All empty paint cans to be removed but part full paint cans to be left for future touch up with paint name visible.

Flooring

Installed wood flooring as selected by the customer in accordance with manufacturers' installation instructions [160 sq. ft.].

Install metal strips where the wood floor meets carpet.

Install prefinished shoe molding at the joint around the baseboard.

Remove all debris. Leave any unused flooring for repairs.

Any doors removed must be re-hung before completion.

Any fitting of doors at the bottom are the responsibility of the flooring contractor at no additional cost.

The above specification is for example only. Write a similar specification for all work and all areas.

Typical Remodel Costs

Additions	Costs
Build addition	$100 to 150 / sq ft
Enclose porch	$7,500 to 16,000
Deck 16 by 20	$10,000 to 13,000
Drywall ceiling over plaster	$1.50 to 2.00 / sq ft
Basement	**Costs**

Convert basement to living space inc bathroom	$28,000 to 50,000
Bathroom	**Costs**
Remodel Guest bathroom	$7,000 to 15,000
Remodel Master bathroom	$12,000 to 30,000
Remodel Powder room [sink & toilet]	$2,000 to 3,000
Electrical	**Costs**
Increase service to 200 amps	$900 to 1,900
Run separate electrical lines	$200 to 350
Add recessed Lighting – per can	$100 to 200
Rewire complete house	$3,000 to 5,000
Exterior	**Costs**
Re sod lawn [2,000 sq ft]	$1,000
Replace siding	$5 to 7 / sq ft
Replace stucco	$6 to 9 / sq ft
Paint siding/stucco & trim	$2,000 to 4,000
Fence	$12 to 15 / lin ft
Concrete driveway	$5 to 8 / sq ft
Stamped concrete patio	$7 to 20 / sq ft
New gutters and downspouts	$3.50 to 4.50 / lin. ft
Fireplaces	**Costs**

Build masonry fireplace	$4,300 to 5,800
Install prefabricated fireplace	$2,800 to 3,800
Install wood stove [single story]	$2,000 to $3,000

Floors	Costs
Sand and finish wood floors	$1.80 to 3.60 / sq ft
Install hardwood flooring [plus material]	$7 to 11 / sq ft
Install ceramic tile floor [plus material]	$5 to 10 / sq ft
Install vinyl tile or sheet floor [plus material]	$1 to 2 / sq ft
Install wall-to-wall carpet [plus material]	$2 to 6 / sq yd

Interior	Costs
Install drywall, tape & texture	$30 / sheet
Repair drywall, & match texture	$500 / room
Paint walls, ceilings & wood trim	$1,000 to 2,000
Add baseboard / door trim	$0.65 to 0.90 / lin ft
Add crown molding per room	$8 to 12 / lin ft

Garages	Costs
Build single car garage	$8,000 to 9,500

Build double car garage	$10,000 to 14,000
Replace garage door - double	$600 to 1,600
Heating and Air Conditioning	**Costs**
New central air conditioning system (electric)	$3,500 to 4,000
New central air conditioning system (gas)	$4,000 to 4,500
Add to above if new ducts are needed	$3,000 to 4,000
Install attic ventilation	$280 to 460
Insulation	**Costs**
Insulate attic / basement	$.85 to 1.40 / sq ft
Kitchen	**Costs**
Remodel kitchen upgrading existing cabinets	$10,000 and up
Remodel kitchen complete replacement	$15,000 and up
Plumbing	**Costs**
Hot water heater 40 gal electric	$400 to $500
Hot water heater 40 gal gas	$450 to $550
Install new septic system	$4,000 to 7,000
Install sump pump	$420 to 520
Install French drain and sump pump	$3,000 to 4,500

Roofs	Costs
Asphalt / fiberglass shingles-	
Install over existing shingles	$1.50 to 3.70 / sq ft
Remove existing shingles and install new	$2.60 to 4.25 / sq ft
Windows & Doors	**Costs**
Replace front door	$800 to 1,400
Interior door	$200 to 300
Replace patio door with French doors	$1,500 to 2,650
Replace windows low E dual pane vinyl	$350 to 700 each

This table is just a guide based on 2008. Actual costs will depend on the part of the country, quality of materials and the experience of the contractor.

Address			City		
HOA yes / no	Sq Ft		Beds	Bat hs	Ag e
Property asking price $		Offer price $		Accepted price $	
Comp High $		Comp Low $		Comp Average $	
Work	**Size /#**	**Uni t Cos t**	**Tot al cos t**		
Roofing sq ft					
Exterior					
Windows & Doors					
Demo					
Kitchen					
Bathroom s					
Plumbing					
Electrical					
HVAC					
Drywall wall & ceiling area					
Paint & décor					

Tile sq ft					
Floor coverings sq ft					
Permits					
Landscap ing					
Addition sq ft					
Total cost of work					
Purchase price					
Purchase expenses					
Realtor fees					
Closing cost					
15% emergency					
Total cost of project					
Projected selling price					

Appendix

FORMS

Move-In & Move-Out Rental Inspection

Address					
Inspection date	Move-In		Move-Out		
Codes SC=Scratched	=Good B=Broken	F=Fair D=Dirty	P=Poor X=None	M=Missing ST=Stained	
	M o v e - I n		**M o v e - O u t**		
	Code	Comments	Code	Comments	
Living Room					
Ceiling, Walls & Trim					
Flooring					
Window & Screen					
Door					
Light					
Outlets & Switch					
Other					
Kitchen					
Ceiling, Walls & Trim					
Flooring					
Window & Screen					
Light					
Cabinets					
Counter					
Sink & Faucet					
Stove clean & working					
Fridge clean & working					
Garbage Disposal					
Dishwasher					
Other					
Bed Room 1					
Ceiling, Walls & Trim					
Flooring					
Window & Screen					
Doors					
Light					
Smoke Det. working					
Bed Room 2					
Ceiling, Walls & Trim					
Flooring					
Window & Screen					
Doors					
Light					
Smoke Det. working					

Bed Room 3				
Ceiling, Walls & Trim				
Flooring				
Window & Screen				
Doors				
Light				
Smoke Det. working				
Bathroom 1				
Ceiling, Walls & Trim				
Flooring				
Window & Screen				
Door				
Toilet				
Sink				
Tub & Shower				
Bathroom 2				
Ceiling, Walls & Trim				
Flooring				
Window & Screen				
Door				
Toilet				
Sink				
Tub & Shower				
Exterior				
Siding & Trim				
Paint				
Gutters & Downpipes				
Windows				
Doors				
Walkways				
Grass & Shrubs				
Shed / Garage				
Signed Landlord		X		
	date	signed		
Signed Tenant		X		
	date	signed	date	signed

Rental Disclosure

The law requires certain forms be provided to the tenant on move-in to a Rental

[   ]   Lead-Based paint brochure

OR

[   ]   Property built after 1978 so this brochure is not required

[   ]   Mold Brochure Provided

[   ]   All smoke detectors are working when I move in and I agree to keep fresh batteries fitted

[   ]   A working carbon monoxide detector is fitted and I agree to keep a fresh battery fitted

I certify the above documents have been provided and the smoke detectors and carbon monoxide detector is working.

_____

Signed   dated

Made in the USA
Coppell, TX
04 February 2021

49559722R00176